D0722244

Ms. Goes to College

ms goes to College

Jean Glidden Henderson
Algo D. Henderson

SOUTHERN ILLINOIS UNIVERSITY PRESS
Carbondale and Edwardsville

Feffer & Simons, Inc.
London and Amsterdam

Library of Congress Cataloging in Publication Data

Henderson, Jean Glidden
    Ms. goes to college.

    Bibliography: p.
    Includes index.
    1.   Higher education of women--United States.
2.   College students--Conduct of life.   I.   Henderson,
Algo Donmyer   joint author.   II,   Title.
LC1567.H46   378.1'98   74–26679
ISBN 0–8093–0699–9
ISBN 0–8093–0713–8 pbk.

Chapter 13, "The Anatomy of Sex," from *The Student Guide to Sex on Campus* by Dr.
Philip Sarrel. Copyright © 1971 by Dr. Philip Sarrel. Reprinted by arrangement with The
New American Library, Inc., New York, New York.

To Carol, Joanne, and Philip

Contents

vi

Preface

WE GOT the idea for this book in talking with college students. One of the things we kept hearing was, "I wish I had known this or that when I was a freshman." So we wrote this book for young women in college or planning to go. The purpose is to give information, and also ideas, pro and con, on the problems they face.

If you are one of these young women, how do you decide upon a college and the courses that you should take there? What should you study to become a well-educated person? How can you discover interesting courses? Experiences? What careers are open to women and how can you identify one to study for? How should you resolve the problem of marriage and also having a career?

How can a college help you to find out more about yourself—who you are? How shall you manage your sex life? The drug scene?

What does college mean to a woman who wants to be liberated?

We gratefully acknowledge assistance from the Exxon Education Foundation and the Center for Research and Development in Higher Education, the University of California, Berkeley. We appreciate having been given access to fresh data about college women that were collected by the study, "School to College: Opportunities for Post-Secondary Education" (SCOPE), and by the Carnegie Commission on Higher Education; also permission by Philip Sarrel, M.D., and the New American Library to use a portion of Chapter 1 of *The Student Guide to Sex on*

Campus. We wish to thank Dr. Bernice Sandler, Henry B. Bruyn, M.D., Joel Fort, M.D., Ms. Mildred Henry, and Ms. Harriet Renaud for reading and criticizing certain chapters, and Ms. Cecilia Bartholomew for counsel and editorial help.

It was a rewarding experience to interview in depth a considerable number of young women of college age and a few mothers. They gave us valuable insights into the problems being met by college-age youth. Where we have used statements from these interviews we have endeavored to assure anonymity, but also to relate faithfully the substance of what was said.

Jean Glidden Henderson
Algo D. Henderson

October 15, 1974
Berkeley, California

Ms. Goes to College

All That Freedom

IN college every woman student bumps up against certain problems—what she studies, whether to prepare for a career or for marriage or for both. What kind of a career or job she would like to have. How to make plans with her boyfriend. Should she have sex? What about social causes—what is truth and what is propaganda? Can she influence what happens? What are the best courses for her to take, both cultural and vocational? Most of all she wants to know who she is, what type and quality of life she wants to live, and how to use her time in college to prepare for this life.

If you are a college student, you will face some of these problems, perhaps all of them. Your possible choices on many things—sex, career, life-style, for example, are different from those of your mother's generation. You have new freedoms now which give you advantages and opportunities but which also expose you to risks and impose more decisions on you. Today you may seriously consider careers that heretofore were open only to men. The opportunity in such fields may be better for you than in an occupation populated mainly by women. And the work is probably more interesting, too. But be aware also what discriminations toward women continue to exist in some fields. You may live with a man without being married and not receive the same degree of social disapproval women met just a few years ago. But living together means having sex, and if you are to reduce the risks, know your body and have full information about contraception and pregnancy.

As a woman in college, you are contending with three identities: sexual, intellectual, and professional or occupational. Tradition has claimed that the last two are sex-linked, but modern research asserts that this is not so. Formerly women could separate these identities. If she lived up to social expectations her motivations would be toward marriage and a life devoted to her home and family, and that was it. Or she might, if she were extremely determined, eschew marriage and persevere in her studies to a profession. You may decide to do either of these or neither. But the chances are that you will be working outside your home for twenty or more years of your life. Moreover, today, as a liberated woman, you may want to have and enjoy all three identities. You may take time out to begin a family and later return to work or to a career after your children have entered school. If this is your course, you will find the shift easier to make when the time comes if you prepare for it beforehand. Or you may have a career and not interrupt your work when you have a child or two.

In order to know what problems young women in college face today, we interviewed a number of them. The following are excerpts from some of their conversations.

Ann, a sophomore, was describing why she thought it was important to go away to college: "If I lived at home, I'd never have found out about myself! Even now, my father is always telling me what I should be thinking and how I should behave. You learn so much about yourself if you live away from home. Like learning that you've got to get certain things done, and learning how you tick. Mostly, it's trying to find out what you think is right and wrong. At first I did the opposite of what I thought my parents would say to do. Now I try very hard to figure out what *I* want to do and how *I* feel about it. Sometimes I worry that I do things to please other people, because you know, I like to be liked. And I wonder, am I doing something for them, or because I like to do it myself?"

Linda, on the other hand, prefers to live at home. The daughter of an army officer, she told us, "I'm glad I could go to college and live at home. My parents give me a lot of freedom, we don't have many problems, we get along pretty well. Besides, I have my own room and a lot of quiet. We moved around so much when my Dad was in the army that it feels good to be home for a while—sort of permanent-like. Of course, I'm lucky that I'm an only child and my parents could afford to send me to any college, but lots of my friends at school couldn't go to college if they had to go away."

Sue told us, "All college women have the problem of sex. We aren't as free as we think we are. We haven't been brought up all our lives with sexual freedom, I know that I personally, no matter how hard I try, cannot think of sex as just recreational sex, you know. It's a very emotional kind of thing. There's a lot of pressure on college campuses to experience sex. It's very hard, just to change like that and to . . . to live with different guys and to go through different sexual scenes when you haven't been brought up like that. On the other hand, we're still being bombarded with the romantic mate and the social pressure kinds of things on TV and in the advertisements, and I don't think women have arrived at equality there.

"But then, it seems like once you've had sexual experiences it's really hard to just turn them off, you know. I'm sure even years ago, women on college campuses were having problems with boyfriends like we are but now it's on a totally different level, because it's a lot more intense than it was twenty-five years ago and I think it has to do with the sexual relationships that are going on. Because you've invested so much in it and you're so emotionally involved."

In an interview with Andrea, a graduate student at Berkeley, we asked her how involved she was with the political issues that seem ubiquitous to the campus. She replied that she became involved after listening to the heated discussions on campus. College students had opinions and wanted them to count. She said: "Here it was, my first quarter on the Berkeley campus, and all of a sudden I had to face the Cambodia issue. And it would have been so much easier if it hadn't arisen. I just couldn't continue going to classes . . . I just felt that there were things that I had to do, and I didn't end up doing very much. When you've given your all to a demonstration and nothing's been changed, the frustration and the let-down you feel!" Andrea's problem is not unusual. How do you sort out the issues and how do you, as a citizen, make your influence felt?

In another interview with two young women, Cindy, a senior, and Margot, a junior, we had been talking about their future plans. Although each was involved in a serious relationship with a young man, neither was considering marriage in the near future. But in discussions of careers and work, they interlaced their discussions of their lives as individuals with their sexual lives.

MARGOT: "I've thought a lot about what kind of work I could do when I graduate. I think that's important. I changed my major and there were a number of things that went into it, but when I was in nursing what I would do wasn't a problem. I felt I could always get a job . . . even a good-paying one . . . as a nurse. But now that I'm majoring in psychology, well, I've seen my roommate, she graduated Phi Beta Kappa, working as a secretary in an insurance firm. And that's pretty real. I know with a B.A. I'm not going to be able to step out there and get any kind of a real job. People are going to look at me and ask me how fast I can type. I'm prepared for that. Those are the kinds of jobs I've had, you know. And they're easy jobs. You don't have to think. And it's good money and all that, I suppose. But is that what I went to college for, to become a typist?"

CINDY: "You know, I have only two more quarters before I graduate, and that's so soon, and I'm really torn, and a lot of it goes beyond what I'll do as a career. I'm realizing that a lot of my goals and my fantasies . . . more like my fantasies, I guess, have always been in the domestic area, and having a boyfriend, I feel also, well, I've done everything I'm supposed to do before I get married. It's perfectly reasonable that I could get married now, and I think I could handle it, but I'm feeling that kind of conflict now . . . the real forever-ness thing. On the other hand, I know that my work is important to me, too, my need to go on to graduate school. I don't think I could be happy not pursuing a career. I can see some good things about marriage . . . it doesn't seem like a totally wasted institution to me; although there are a lot of things that need to be changed I can see that it could work. I have to decide what I'm going to do next fall, after I graduate. I guess Andy is my real problem. Making a decision, no matter how hard I try, is always done with Andy in mind even if it's not to include him. It's very difficult I'm finding. Now to suddenly assert myself and say, 'these are priorities that I have to accomplish myself' . . . I don't know whether I'm ready to do that. I've never had to before. It's a pretty uncomfortable feeling. Besides, if I go to graduate school that will mean I'm serious about a career. How will Andy really feel about his home and career wife? I don't think we talk enough about it. He doesn't seem ready for it this year . . . maybe next year. I always get the feeling that if we talk about it, then I'm asking him to marry me, which is not it at all."

MARGOT: "We're sort of planning, John and I that is, that we may live together when I finish school. I don't feel the need, at least right now, to get married and I would just as soon live with him for a while. I've felt that way for a long time, even before I'd met him I thought that if there was someone whom I thought that I might want to stay with forever, I'd like to live with that person for a while before I got married. My problem is my mother . . . you know how kind of traditional she is . . . old-fashioned, I guess. She thinks you should get engaged, with a ring and all, get married, have a couple of children, keep yourself up for your husband, and that whole scene. My grandmother, now, she has become very liberated. She's sixty-two and she's exposed to younger people because she takes a course in ceramics at the community center. She says now she wishes she had taken ceramics and more of other things like literature and philosophy when she was in college. She gets very upset, because she really sympathizes with the women's movement and she looks back on her life and she just feels awful. She just thinks, here, my whole life has been wasted. I think to myself, sure we've been brought up in the traditional way and yet there's still kind of a new change. We haven't gone into our careers, we haven't done new things, but we still can after we're through school. But when you reach sixty-five or whatever and you look back, it can be a little disheartening, you know, to think of the life you could have had, it could have been better."

These are some of the concerns expressed by students that may or may not be the ones you have. But perhaps this book deals sufficiently comprehensively with problem areas that it can help you. It also endeavors to do some additional things. We are in a period of social change, and among the consequences is a change in woman's place and woman's role. These changes have greatly affected the opportunities for women in college. In the past, women have permitted men to define their roles. The woman was a homemaker. When she got married she was expected to be a virgin. When she applied for a job she was discriminated against in the salary and in the type of work that she was given to do. Some men have thought that women had nonintellectual interests, that they could be artistic, but not creative, that they could not do sustained, rigorous, intellectual work such as research. Women have been socialized from early childhood to accept this kind of place relative to men. But these beliefs are shifting, and rapidly. The liberation movement is causing many women to aspire to the same careers and the same freedom in life as men.

Girls do compete and excel in achievement equally with boys in high school. But in college, many women students seem to hold back. This may be because they think they should not appear superior to their male classmates, and especially their boyfriends. Naturally they want to be acceptable companions. But women also have more difficult problems to cope with in college than men do. For example, the dilemma of preparing for both marriage and an occupation bears heavily upon the woman student. She not only has to prepare well, as any man would do, but she must also untangle her thinking because of the indoctrination she received earlier. Problems relating to the life styles of women are more difficult. In sexual relationships it is the woman who becomes pregnant and in whom venereal disease is less easily detected. These are difficult problems. In this book we endeavor to provide you with information to make good choices. We also present the findings from the most recent research to help you to gain self-assurance about the wisdom of your decisions. We aim to reduce your anxieties about such problems so that you can apply your intelligence more fully in college.

Our thesis is that college can be a liberating experience. For one thing, it is the college's objective (among others) to teach you how to think clearly and to use various methods by which you may develop your reasoning power. Of course, practice in the kind of careful reasoning that should take place in the classroom and laboratory, or in discussing a problem with a professor, improves your skills and your habits of thinking.

While in college you have the time and the opportunity to explore how the courses and the educative experiences can be liberating for you. Almost every college has two thrusts to its curriculum—vocational and general or liberal education. At college both can be explored simultaneously. For that is the way life is—most people want to work and also to do things with cultural and community interests that lead to a richer life.

2

Struggle for
Intellectual Freedom

OT so long ago American women literally had to force their way into college. The Michigan state law, for example, required that the university should be open to all persons resident in the state; yet for fifty years after its founding the regents of the University of Michigan barred women. Weren't women persons? The regents did not admit persons who were moral risks and no one had questioned their authority to exclude them. Hence it could be reasoned the law clearly did not mean that the university had to admit *all* persons. In any event, the regents decided that women should not be admitted. The university just didn't want women, period.

A few glimpses into the past will provide us with a perspective on the problems of women in college today. Within three or four generations women have moved from hoopskirts to miniskirts, from protected virginity to communal sex, and from being dilettantes to being intellectuals.

Oberlin College is usually credited with having opened the doors of college to women. Organized in 1833, in 1837 Oberlin accepted four women at the college level. The college prepared a special "Ladies Course," and at the beginning women enrolled in it rather than in the degree course. Antioch College in 1853 admitted all women to its regular course, and in addition, even permitted them to sit with the men on the commencement platform. Georgia Female College, a successor to a female seminary of similar name, is credited by some authors as having been given the first chartered authority (1836) to grant degrees to women. The first state university to admit women was Iowa (1856). Vassar College became a model for the separate women's college with collegiate standards, but it did not enroll students until 1865—just after the Civil War.

Women did not jump suddenly from no education to higher education. Throughout recorded history there have been exceptional women who educated themselves or were tutored. The predecessor of the female college was the female seminary, in some senses a secondary school but better described as a finishing school. The purpose of the seminary was to prepare young ladies for their domestic and social responsibilities. Hence, the emphasis was upon morals, manners, and domestic arts. Considering the functions of women of the time—maintaining the home, bearing children, spinning yarn and weaving cloth, playing the piano, influencing their sons in moral behavior, and providing social entertainment—one cannot quarrel with the relevance of their instruction in the seminary.

To return to Michigan, the regents of the university were faced with a genuine dilemma. From a rational and a legal view, it was clear that women should be admitted to the university. Also, by this time there was considerable precedent for the action and experience upon which to make the judgment. On the other hand, all custom relating to women and their role and all tradition in formal intellectual training were opposed to the idea. So in 1857 the regents made a special study of this controversial subject. The study included inquiries addressed to prominent educators of the time.

The opinion of President Walker of Harvard was sought. He reminded the regents that there existed an "immense preponderance of enlightened public opinion" against the experiment, and he said that he fully concurred in it. President Woolsey of Yale wrote: "Of what use degrees are to be to girls I don't see, unless they addict themselves to professional life." That was clearly unthinkable except in the minds of a few. As of 1850 there were no women lawyers, no women physicians, no women journalists, no women librarians, no women architects.

President Nott of Union College also responded to the inquiry from the regents. He pointed out that the education of women and men, respectively, had opposite goals; so how could they be mixed? Women required "delicacy of sentiment, a feeling of dependence, and shrinking from the public view," whereas the attributes of men were "decision of character, self-reliance, a feeling of personal independence, and a willingness to meet opposition and encounter difficulties." This thesis was to be repeated by educators many times during the next several decades.

It was only from two colleges, Oberlin and Antioch, that messages of encouragement came to the Michigan regents. President Charles G. Finney of Oberlin reported that with them the results of coeducation were quite satisfactory and even admirable. President Horace Mann of Antioch wrote with enthusiasm about the experiment there. Mann advanced two cogent arguments: one, that women had as good a right as men to higher education, and two, that both could be educated better and cheaper together. He thought that coeducation was good for the men as it refined their manners. As for the women, the actual daily association with men and knowledge of their character "has a strong tendency to expel all girlish romance and to exorcise the miserable nonsense which comes from novel reading."

But Mann then discussed at great length the problem of preserving the virtue of the women students. He said that the dangers of coeducation were "terrible," but added that at Antioch "we never have had here the happening of one of those events mildly called accidents, but it is only because of our constant sleepless vigilance." He proceeded to offer several points of advice: Do not let them "board promiscuously" in the village; let men and women eat together, as it is inducive to refinement of manners, but then separate them; insure against clandestine meetings, and also clandestine correspondence; have both president and faculty "exercise vigilance over the girls" as conscientiously as they would over their own daughters. President Finney of Oberlin also gave advice along the same line. He suggested appointing a wise and pious matron, maintaining a powerful religious influence and cultivating the surrounding community to sustain the regulations of the university concerning moral conduct.

As a result of their study, the regents of the University of Michigan concluded that to accommodate women with the kind of program they should have would require a revolution in the organization of the university so vast as not to be feasible to undertake. The answer to women once again was "no." It wasn't that women should not be educated, but it was crucial for the future of mankind that they have the right kind of education. It was "for the sake of the young ladies themselves" that they should not enter this university, said the regents. Some might pass the "trying ordeal unharmed," yet as a class "they would lose more than they would gain." But women kept knocking on the Michigan door and finally, in 1870, it was opened.

The fear on the part of college educators for the future of the human race if women were to receive the same education as men was supported by certain medical authority. Women had always engaged in much physical labor. If now they went without exercise, sitting for hours while studying, they would become puny and nervous and this would impede their milk supply and interfere with the nursing of babies. The influential philosopher, Herbert Spencer, said that "absolute or relative infertility is commonly produced in women by mental labor carried to excess." As a result the best stocks in society might become sterilized. The educated woman might also resist marriage. One author, Dr. Edward H. Clarke (1873), carrying the prestige of having been on the Harvard medical faculty, argued seriously that if women in the United States became overeducated the men should send to Europe for wives. Dr. Clarke's book, *Sex and Education,* required seventeen editions to satisfy the demand for it. Also, if the educated woman did marry, what would be the value of her education? She couldn't use it while washing diapers, so her education would have been a waste of time and money.

But a more potent argument lay in the grave doubt as to whether women could really do sustained, rigorous intellectual work. A contributing factor was their tendency to be more or less sick for one-quarter of each month. G. Stanley Hall, an eminent psychologist, thought that menstruation would be unfavorably affected by rigorous, intellectual effort. Even in the twentieth century, Bowdoin's President William D. Hyde stated that "productive scholarship should remain and will remain in man's hands." The president of Stanford, David Starr Jordan (1906), advocated better education for women but believed that "original investigation, creative art, the resolute facing of the world as it is" were the man's domain. This kind of thinking was shared by many women. On the campuses where women were admitted there was no general acceptance of their right to be there. The men students stared and hooted at the new coeds. Older women of the community snubbed them.

Women were, of course, well indoctrinated about their status and role. The ideal of becoming ladylike was attractive to young women. In the more genteel families, the young ladies desired to become accomplished at the piano because this was a mark of culture. Learning to play well required much daily practice. They accepted the necessity in the marital relationship of bearing children, and a dozen or so babies arriving at two-year intervals kept them tied to the home. Prior to 1920, the average life span for women was little more than half of what it is today, and so the bearing of children occupied almost the whole of the prime years of their lives.

Smith College denied the allegations of the day (1897) that its students all wore glasses and masculine collars, or that they talked continuously about women's rights and political issues. Most colleges held teas and receptions, and afternoons at home for women students. They saw themselves fitting women to take their place as true wives and mothers—and in the case of necessity to be self-supporting as teachers.

The colleges were very protective of the young women and continued to be so well into the twentieth century. They posted definite hours for rising, studying, and retiring; they faithfully kept the Sabbath, even, in some institutions, forbidding the writing of compositions or of letters; students had to own a Bible, attend church, and avoid indulging in light or trivial conversations on Sundays; keeping company with young men and corresponding with them was much restricted; chaperons accompanied the young women on calls, and even to the stores downtown; and politeness and due respect were required toward teachers and associates.

It took a long time to shift the programs for women from concerns with personal development and domestic training to those of the liberal arts and of preparation for the professions. Sewing, cooking, reading, conversation, music, moral and religious instruction, and physical education and hygiene continued into the twentieth century and were emphasized as proper for young women. But to French were added the classics and also German and Italian. The study of history by women expanded at a leisurely pace but it did expand and presently the subject became an elaborate array of courses. Literature also came to the fore. Mathematics, natural philosophy, astronomy, and chemistry began to come into the picture. Chemistry was adapted for women by training them in food analysis, sanitation, and industrial chemistry; English was used to train creative writers and the natural sciences to prepare research personnel. Later, the biological sciences were assumed to be relevant to women's interests and work. By the time the social sciences came in as disciplines, both women and men were ready for them.

A few women graduates sought to be librarians, social workers, and institutional managers. Many women, however, found most occupations closed to them. In their desire to secure employment following the receipt of their bachelor's degrees, they enrolled in the private business colleges to learn typing and stenography. After 1920, secretarial work became second only to teaching as a career for college-educated women. The employment of women as public school teachers was a breakthrough for women as it was the first bridge to the professions. Courses in professional education for teaching began to be offered in many colleges and universities. Schools of law and of medicine began to admit a few women. At the University of Michigan, in spite of earlier opposition from the faculty, women in the medical curriculum rose to between 20 and 25 percent of the student group during the period 1880 to 1900. Unfortunately, in subsequent decades the image of the physician as a male became so strong that the percentage of females at Michigan and other medical schools declined to a small figure. The same situation applied in law and the ministry. Not until 1970 was there a material shift of attitude in favor of women as students in these professions.

Women leaders of the nineteenth and early twentieth centuries continued to press for equal treatment with men. Fortunately, economic, social, and religious trends developed in their favor. The beliefs of men that had been based on earlier economic, social, and religious concepts, and upon presumptions about the physical limitations and the intellectual interests and abilities of women, were being undermined. They were being shown up as mere prejudice, an urge to protect their own interests, or at best, plain ignorance.

Perhaps the most potent of the trends was the advance of the industrial revolution. The mechanized factory took over the manufacturing role of the woman in the home. No longer did she need to make clothing and can great quantities of fruits and vegetables. Later, she was freed from churning butter and baking bread. The factory could do these things more efficiently and economically. Furthermore, since women accepted employment at lower wages than men they were able to get jobs and share the wage earning with the husband. The historic separation of duties—women in the home, men outside—became disrupted.

The democratic beliefs of men, strongly influential following the French and American revolutions, caused the spread of egalitarianism. Political leaders argued that if men were to govern they had to be literate. And so evolved the concept of the public school to teach men—and women—to read, write, and do arithmetic. With the growth of the public school system—and it spread rapidly in the United States—arose also the need for teachers. Women could teach in the elementary school, so it was thought, and they could be employed more cheaply than men. This occupation also took them out of the home. From their beginning the normal schools, which trained teachers, admitted women.

As the theory of evolution became supported by massive evidence, the decline of dogmatism in religion brought changes in the religious impact. Religious fundamentalism had had a firm grip on America. The great Presbyterian, John Knox, had declared that woman was made to serve and obey man, not to rule and command him. Every bride promised to love, honor, and obey her husband. But the new science challenged many religious beliefs and the effect on our culture was profound. The scientific method as a way of learning principles of human behavior became a tool for women as well as for men.

The biological concerns about the effects of education upon women were proving to have been myths. Education not only did not hinder the marital relationships, but the educated men began to choose educated women as their life partners. In 1906, President Jordan of Stanford, defending coeducation, wrote that the normal girl remains normal, does not become upon graduation asthenic, anaemic, neurotic, or indifferent to love and maternity. "The mental activity necessary to a successful college course is not intense enough to interfere with fecundity," he declared. The transfer of the home chores to the factory coupled with the introduction of gas and electric power into the kitchen brought much freedom of time for girls after puberty and before marriage. The age of marriage was extended from the teens into the twenties. The practice of birth control as a means of planning the family helped to release women from the imprisonment of the home. These events converged to create time that could be spent in high school and college.

As the energies of women flowed more and more outside the home, women began to take deep interest in public life. They wanted the schools to be good schools, government to be responsible government, hospitals to be adequately staffed and to have good facilities. Thus their own attitudes toward their role changed, influencing them to be more persuasive with the men. Wyoming in 1869 broke the ice on suffrage by granting the vote to women. Fifty years later the nation followed suit.

Jobs, cultural activities, and civic and political participation prompted a demand for more education, for higher education—for women the same as for men. Today women may enter college freely. They seek entrance to college on the same terms as men in order to educate themselves, to gain access to the professions, to participate equally in civic affairs, to achieve intellectual freedom.

Which College
for You?

IANE was feeling pretty low. Oakline College had turned into a disaster!

Her high school art teacher had said she thought it was a good school. Her friend Karen knew someone who had attended Oakline for a while and said it was a great place. For one thing, you could live your own life, no one ever hassled you about dope or dogs on campus. Diane had looked over a folder which the college had sent to her. They had still been accepting applications, which was good, since Diane had put off making a decision about college until August, a month before the term began. She had wanted to go away to college and to study art. Oakline seemed to be the perfect answer, four hundred miles from home and offering a major in arts and crafts. It was a small college, yet certainly not parochial. It offered the promise of all the good things she wanted out of college.

Now that she was here, she realized that size was relative—how many bodies could the campus hold? Right now there were about three hundred too many. Classes were small only when they met in small rooms, and there weren't very many small ones. The provisions for doing art work were just too meager. It was no wonder that classes became smaller and smaller as the term progressed. The liberal arts courses were a waste of time—her high school classes had contained more intellectual content. Oakline lauded its individualized instruction, but Diane found a laissez-faire indifference rather than any real guidance of independent work. There was a pervasive air of expediency about the college. Nobody seemed to care much about anybody else. The instructors criticized the administration and each other.

Diane arrived at her eight o'clock on time, and now it was twenty minutes after. The instructor didn't show up again—the third time this month. The students who had come to class sat there disconsolately, griping. Diane left for breakfast. On her return to her dormitory room she found that the canvases she had just bought for her painting class had been ripped off. That was the last straw! Diane rushed up to the student affairs office in tears. The man who was in charge, a retired army colonel, hadn't arrived yet—he would be in sometime between ten and twelve, no one was quite sure. She was advised to write out a report of her problem and leave it for him. She exclaimed, "I want to see someone now! Why do you publicize academic and personal counseling if there isn't any?"

"How did I get myself into such a mess?" Diane asked herself.

It was a good question. For one thing, some college brochures, particularly those of the mediocre private colleges, describe dream campuses. They aim for the ideal presented by the prestige colleges. They speak of their small classes and concerned faculty, of each student being guided into developing her fullest potential, while the actuality is often different. On the other hand, not all small colleges are mediocre. Some may be very good. Diane did not spend enough time on selecting her college—she probably spends more time deciding on a new pair of shoes than she did deciding on which college to attend. Early planning with enough time to learn something about the school can prevent your wasting your time and money as Diane did.

Another reason for beginning your plans for college early in your high school career is that some liberal arts colleges have specific requirements in college preparatory courses for admission. If you wait until you are a senior you may have insufficient time to complete them. Some institutions may require entrance tests, either their own or those administered by the College Entrance Examination Board or the American College Testing Service which are given at specified times during the year. Furthermore, preprofessional programs such as those for medicine, engineering, architecture, and others, may require sequences of science or mathematics in high school. Or a college may consider accepting good students if they have superior records after three years of high school.

This is not general practice, but has been done on an individual basis.

There are two-year colleges, four-year colleges, universities, and public and private institutions; undoubtedly, you know this. But are you sufficiently informed about the great diversity that exists? Perhaps one type will meet your special needs better than the others. First, how do they differ?

Universitites differ from colleges in that in addition to the undergraduate college or colleges offering liberal arts (general education) and pre-professional programs, they generally offer graduate work and include one or more professional schools such as medicine, law, engineering, and social work. A university, in essence, is a group of colleges, undergraduate and graduate.

The characteristic college is usually a four-year liberal arts undergraduate institution offering a broad general education, with a variety of fields of concentration or majors, leading to a bachelor's degree. Students who do not have a clear vocational goal in mind cannot go wrong by enrolling in a liberal arts course. Moreover, like universities, colleges can prepare a student to enter a professional school. Indeed, many professional schools—education, architecture, pharmacy, and so forth, require two years or more of general education before admission.

Junior or community colleges may be public or private and usually have an "open door" admissions policy. This means minimal entrance requirements. The public junior colleges offer two years of general education (the college transfer curriculum) and a variety of technical and vocational programs. Private junior colleges usually offer either liberal arts or specializations in one or more fields. In most public community colleges, it is possible to attend full or part time either during the day or at night.

In addition there are colleges which offer special programs. For example, there are about six hundred colleges that offer cooperative work-study programs where students attend classes for a term or a year and then work for a specified time in a job which supplements their classroom work. These programs vary in type from work-study interrelationships in technical fields, such as engineering and business administration, to a few that are based on the liberal arts, as at Antioch College. Some of the colleges emphasize the opportunity to earn money while attending college; others seek to add a dimension to the education of the student. Programs which are problem-oriented instead of solely textbook theory are offered by some colleges. There are four-year institutions which specialize in areas such as music, religion, dramatics, teacher education, and so forth. Still another category is the post–high school vocation - training school, of which there usually are one or more in every medium or large-sized city. Then there are colleges that have gone outside the traditional campus using the community for their resources. These colleges are usually identified as experimental, new, or colleges without walls. The curriculum is tailored to the individual student. It may be the study of social problems or it can be independent study including library research under the guidance of faculty advisers. Some programs include tutorial work. They can be good or poor depending upon the dedication, direction, and creative intelligence of the planners and the faculty. Some offer substantial in-depth study, more concentrated than that offered in the traditional classroom; others are schools for goof-offs.

There are over 2600 colleges and universities in the United States and its outlying areas. Since they are all different from each other in some way and vary in quality and character, how do you reduce this number to a manageable size in order to consider and investigate institutions you may want to attend? Your first concern will probably be the overall character of the institution. Do you want a church-related college or one that is nonsectarian? A public or a private institution? Some people have strong opinions about attending one kind of college or the other.

Church-related colleges are small and medium-sized; only the universities, such as Fordham or Southern Methodist, are large. A goodly proportion of the students in a church-related college will probably belong to the religious denomination controlling the college, although in the last ten or twenty years, many of these schools have made efforts to seek a more diversified enrollment. These colleges often have parietal regulations, and the colleges connected with the fundamentalist religions will have definite beliefs about what is proper moral behavior; they are generally not supportive of the changing status of women. They are, by and large, conservative, and maintainers of the status quo.

The independent private colleges of the Radcliffe, Oberlin, and Reed type, are often outstanding in their academic programs. They allow students a large amount of independence. They also have restricted enrollments and are expensive.

Public institutions, because of their size, are often able to offer more diversity in programs and courses than private institutions. Most public colleges are less paternalistic than the private colleges. They may be free, or have low tuition. A mediocre public college or university is to be sought over a mediocre private one, since the public one is apt to have higher salaries and hence can attract better qualified instructors. Once you have decided on the character of the college your list of institutions will be cut in half. Each following decision will further narrow the field.

What about costs? If your money is limited and your chances for securing a scholarship remote, the least costly way to get a college education is to attend your local junior or community college. Your family's taxes have been paying for it, after all, and this is a way of getting a return. If there is tuition, it is nominal, and most students work part time to get carfare and money for lunch and books. Many of its programs require only two years to complete. If you are working toward a bachelor's degree, you can transfer to the state university or other senior college for your final two years. If this is your road, find out which courses transfer and what grades are required, and keep this in mind when selecting your courses at the junior college. In general, the tuition at a private college is much higher than at a public institution. Students from out of state, however, pay high tuition even at public colleges. Don't overlook the loans that are available—private, state, and federal—to help you secure an education. Ask your high school or college counselor about them, write to the U.S. Department of Health, Education, and Welfare in Washington, D.C., to the State Education Department of your state and to your representative in Congress. If you are a top student, or from a seriously disadvantaged family, look into scholarships.

Thirdly, you will consider size. Do you like large groups, different kinds of people, big-city atmosphere? Large universities have this atmosphere on campus. They also have the advantage of being able to offer a variety of programs and activities. Each department can offer many different courses. There will be an array of cultural events and a diverse student population. There may be outstanding scholars on the faculty of a large university, but you may be taught by novices—the new instructors and the graduate assistants. Size is not stimulating to everyone. Being one of thousands—a computer number—robs some people of their feeling of individuality; they are lost and insignificant in a crowd. Perhaps you bloom in a small intimate environment where you will be in contact with people who know you by name, where you will become more closely acquainted with your instructors, as well as the students. Your classes will be taught by ranking professors and may be small in size. A small college also gives you wider opportunities to participate in extracurricular activities: dramatics, athletics, chorus, school paper, and so forth. On the other hand, there is the possibility of finding yourself stagnating on a campus with little outside stimulation or with limited offerings in your major. Find out about this before you go.

What about location? Do you want to remain close to your home (the carfare going home for vacations will be cheaper) or far away? How far? Do you want to be on the east coast, the west coast, the south, the midwest, the mountain states? Do you work best in warm climates or cold? For relaxation, do you like to ski or to swim?

Are your reasons for going to college nonprofessional ones? For education *per se,* for cultural reasons, or for self-fulfillment? In this case, you will select a liberal arts college, whether independent or a unit of a large university. The liberal arts college offers a broad general and cultural education with courses in subjects such as English, art, history, biology, sociology, psychology, music, literature, foreign languages, chemistry, and so forth. It also prepares students for later entrance into graduate or professional school.

Do you have a specific goal in mind? The community college offers technical or vocational courses whereas the liberal arts college offers various special fields and preprofessional courses. The difference is that one is practical and the other requires a theoretical foundation. The vocational courses offered through the two-year colleges are called "terminal" because they prepare a person for a specific occupation. These may be in technology, in paramedical fields, or in fields such as real estate, apparel design, and so forth. There are also two-year programs which prepare for mid-management positions. The four-year colleges, on the other hand, lay the groundwork for the later training in the professions of medicine, law, architecture, engineering, chemistry, psychology, and so forth. The four-year colleges offer at least two years of general education and in addition courses that will give you a degree of mastery in one field, such as literature, history, psychology, economics, chemistry, biology, anthropology, and many others.

If you want to be a musician, or a chemist, or other specialist either in the arts or the sciences, you will want to know if the program or school has professional accreditation. Professional accreditation is in addition to the regional accreditation that is granted to schools meeting certain criteria. Are the colleges on your list of possibilities accredited? If they are, this does not assure you of a quality education, but it tells you whether members of similar institutions think that the college can meet its purposes by the facilities, programs, and faculty that it has. Some colleges, such as newly established ones, may be working toward accreditation; others may be too poorly equipped or financed to secure accreditation. Some may be satisfactory for your needs although not accredited. Occasionally a new college will have an innovative program that may appeal to you. On the other hand, watch out for the fraudulent college. A college can apply for regional accreditation as soon as its plans are laid, but such application does not assure eventual accreditation. Some colleges have been known to announce that they have been accredited when only an application has been made.

If you decide on a nonaccredited college, find out why it is not accredited. (All states require state approval before a school can operate, which is different from being accredited by a regional accrediting association and should not be confused with it.) If your plans include attending graduate school, you will be accepted more readily from an accredited undergraduate college. Also, credit for courses taken at an accredited college is more easily obtained when transferring.

Educational directories include information on accreditation, as well as location of institution, type of control, enrollment figures, sex of student body (women, men, coed, or coordinate), and programs offered. Sources of information on colleges and universities that can be found in your high school guidance office or the public library are: *Educational Directory of Higher Education* issued by the U.S. Department of Health, Education, and Welfare; and the *American Universities and Colleges,* and *American Junior Colleges,* published by the American Council on Education. Other directories to consult are: *The New York Times Guide to College Selection* (well-organized by required test scores, size, tuition, and so forth); *Barron's Profiles of American Colleges* (see particularly the in-depth reports of the colleges you are considering); *Comparative Guide to American Colleges* (good for describing academic pressure, among other facts); and *Lovejoy's College Guide* (includes a handy section which lists by state and specialty the accredited institutions where the programs are offered). Directories in the second group give additional information that is not offered in the institution's literature, such as academic climate, personal qualities of the students, what they wear, and the general atmosphere of the campus. By consulting several directories in addition to the college's catalog, you can gather a great deal of information about an institution.

As a source of supplementary information, seek out the representatives the colleges send to high schools to talk to students. Their visits during "college days" or "career nights" offer you an occasion to obtain initial or additional information and to ask questions that are not answered in the literature of the institutions.

Now that you think that you know which college you want to attend, and you have learned all you can from brochures, catalogs, and directories, there is still something else to do. Would you rent an apartment without seeing it first? Not usually. Then try to visit the college you think you have decided upon during a regular school day before you make your final decision. When on campus, ask to visit some classes. How do the faculty and students feel about each other? Is there mutual respect? What is the campus spirit? Are the students interested in social problems? Are they expectant and enthusiastic or lethargic and frustrated? What is the intellectual climate of the college? Is it vigorous? Will it be too demanding of you? Or will you be bored and feel you are wasting your time? Visit the library and check over a subject you know something about in the card catalog. Are there students in the library making use of it? Are you considering majoring in science? If so, inspect the laboratories. Does the college seem to have good equipment? Visit the cafeteria and talk to the students. Stay overnight in one of the dormitories if possible.

In addition to the informal reports from students, get the formal views of the college by making an appointment with a representative. Ask about the student body: How many freshmen stay to graduate? How many drop out the first year? What is the socioeconomic background? Are there minority groups and how are they treated? How many students are on scholarships and receiving financial aid? Is a profile of the recent entering freshman class available to be consulted?

Another decision you will have to make concerns living arrangements. Where and how you live is important. Should you live at home or on campus? This answer will depend in part on your finances and how secure you will feel to be away from home your first year of college. Living on campus you have a great deal of freedom. Can you manage this independence so that you can get your work done, get up for early classes, and say "no" to dates when they interfere with your obligations?

If you live away from home, dormitory living provides a wide assortment of people from whom you can choose friends. Your own apartment will give you quiet and privacy but also decreases your opportunities to meet people, and you can be lonely at times. Upperclass students advise living on campus for the first year or two for the friendships and mutual support that students who live together give each other. They believe living in a dorm gives you the time and the companionship to discuss your problems and your ideas about life in give-and-take rap sessions that are not possible living alone or at home. It can be a maturing experience and one that helps you to get to know yourself.

Finally the time comes when you have gathered all the information you can from your library investigation, your counselor, your parents, your teachers, your friends, and your personal conversations and visits. You have discussed your choices with your family and are in agreement that the colleges on your list are possible ones. You will discuss your shortened list with your high school counselor who knows a lot about you and about the colleges you are considering. Then the final decision is yours. Apply to the colleges that you want to attend, and when the responses come in, accept the college that is your preference. Do not select a college to please someone else. *You* are the college student.

Study What?

O you know what you want to study in college? If so, you have clear sailing ahead. However, there are many reasons—limited experiences, the intensity of your peer associations, the socialization you have had about woman's place, and the kind and quality of education you got in high school—why your planning might well be reviewed. Do you want to test your planning to see if it is really the best for you? Do you want to clarify your thinking about what you should study?

One way to do this is to consider what other women of your age think and do about planning for themselves. In a nationwide survey of the freshman women in 326 representative colleges and universities (American Council on Education [ACE], 1971) the students were asked to rate in the order of importance each of several possible reasons for going to college. The results were as follows:

Reasons	Percent
Learn more about my interests	73.9
Get a better job	70.1
Gain a general education	66.8
Meet new/interesting people	55.3
Make more money	41.5
Become more cultured	34.0
Prepare for graduate or professional school	29.3

23

Reasons	Percent
Parents wanted me to go	24.1
Contribute more to my community	23.1
Nothing better to do	2.3

In another poll of student opinion (Center for Research and Development in Higher Education, University of California, Berkeley [SCOPE], 1970) 5374 freshman women were asked to define the importance to them of each of several objectives for their college education. The resulting preferences were as follows:

Reasons	Percent
Develop independence in my thinking and behavior	92.6
Develop confidence in taking a stand on things I believe in	88.3
Develop a direction for career or life's work	84.6
Develop skills directly applicable to a career	79.2
Develop intellectual interests and appreciation of ideas	78.9
Develop a satisfying philosophy of life	73.1

A poll of a sample of 190 undergraduate college women (Carnegie Commission on Higher Education [Carnegie], 1969–70) produced answers that agreed with these studies. Women want to achieve independence in thinking, a satisfying philosophy of life, opportunities to be original or creative. They want to become skilled in working with people and in being useful in society. They desire a stable, secure future, and attach importance to finding a career and preparing for it. In one respect, they fall into the woman's traditional role, however. The leadership function is not so important for them.

Among the freshman women in the SCOPE sample, three-fourths expected to attend college for four years or more. About 6 percent, this early in their college career, expected to go as far as a doctoral or professional degree. The portion who expected to achieve a two-year associate degree in arts was 7.5 percent, and those who looked forward to a vocational or technical certificate numbered 10.2 percent. Only a few did not expect a degree of any kind.

In the Carnegie study the women were asked: "Do you think you will drop out before getting a bachelor's degree?" Eighty-five percent said "no," and 35 percent were very positive they would not. These answers differ from what actually happens. The records of the colleges show that women do drop out of college in rather high percentages. The principal reasons are nonacademic: marriage, dissatisfaction with the college environment, changing career plans, finances, reconsideration of interests and goals, and others. Academic failure is not a primary cause; it is eighth on the list.

You have probably thought a great deal about what your major study in college should be. In a community college you may have to make an early decision. This should not be so difficult because so many of the options are for specific job training. Or you may be preparing to transfer to a senior college. If so, you will have time following your admission to the junior college to make up your mind. In senior colleges you normally do not have to make a definite commitment before the beginning of your third year. We present in table 1 data from the SCOPE survey previously referred to. The table offers two kinds of information—the names of the major studies that are common to senior colleges, plus some that relate to preprofessional training; and the number of women who chose each field.

In this survey elementary education attracted the largest interest. The preparation for high school teaching is not shown as a major because those who might have chosen it were distributed among various subject-matter fields. Students may major in elementary education as a means of getting the knowledge and skills requisite for teaching small children, but at the secondary level it is necessary as a prerequisite for teacher certification to become well-prepared in some subject area. The interviewed students later were asked if they planned to go into teaching and, if so, at what level. Twenty percent checked the elementary level and 15 percent the secondary level. Three percent chose the college level. More than one-third responded that they did not plan to teach, and another one-fourth said that at present they were not sure.

It is clear from the table that, after teaching, the more popular fields include health services, the behavioral sciences (psychology, anthropology), business services, music and art, English, and the social sciences. The preferences at the low end of the list—technology, agriculture, engineering, theology, and preparation for law school—are generally regarded as male-oriented and so it is not surprising that the freshman women plan to avoid them. Later, in Chapter 8, we shall discuss some trends that show these fields of employment to be opening to more women.

It may be the safest procedure for you to follow some route that many

1. MAJOR STUDIES OF COLLEGE WOMEN, 1970

Major studies	Number of Women	Percent
Elementary Education	855	15.9%
Medical Technology, Nursing, Allied Health	590	11.0
Behavioral Sciences, such as Psychology, Anthropology, Sociology	585	10.9
Business Services, Clerical, Commercial	547	10.2
Music, Drama, Arts	408	7.6
English, Speech	327	6.1
Social Sciences, such as History, Economics, Political Science	270	5.0
Foreign Languages	197	3.7
Mathematics	180	3.4
Business Administration	170	3.2
Biological Sciences	147	2.8
General Education (Liberal Arts)	146	2.7
Physical Education	128	2.4
Preprofessional, such as Medicine, Dentistry, Pharmacy	123	2.2
Vocational, Trade, Industrial Arts	85	1.6
Philosophy, Humanities	50	.9
Physical Sciences	40	.7
Prelaw	28	.5
Theology, Religion	24	.5
Engineering, Architecture	15	.2
Agriculture, Forestry	12	.2
Technology	9	.2
Other	310	5.8
Don't Know	77	1.4
Unusable answers	51	.9
Totals	5374	100%

Source: SCOPE, 1970.

other women choose. On the other hand, it may work out best for you and perhaps be a more exciting adventure if you make plans that differ from the usual. The first women who, a century and a half ago, demanded admission to college or to medical or law school did that. As a liberated woman you may want to explore carefully the future possibilities in various occupations and professions that heretofore have been marked for men. Or, rather than accept a traditional role, you might like to search for a new or newly developing field.

The socialization defining the place of women that women have experienced when they were young—described in Chapter 9—has left them with views that need to be challenged. For example, some of the impressions received by young women about potential careers are negative. They have been told that women are not good in mathematics and science, and do not have aptitudes for technology. Tests given to women reveal them to be generally strong in verbal skills but weak in technical areas. Could this be a result of their conditioning? Or of the weakness of the tests? In any case, today this has been disproved by many women who have entered industry and the professions, who are successful in the jobs formerly considered the province only of men. The results of those aptitude tests, however, helped to steer women away from mathematics and the sciences and professional fields such as engineering and medicine.

The college experience can be the means of testing these views about oneself as a woman. However, just being a woman rather than a man may influence some choices of what to study. In the chapters that discuss vocations we note that some occupations are female-oriented and others male-oriented. It is also possible that certain cultural courses may appeal to women and others to men. However, differences in college programs for women and men respectively should be minor rather than, as formerly, having programs that are separate and distinct.

All of us are victims of our peer group influences. Because a child stays in her own age group through the twelve grades of school and because television and recreational programs are also attuned to age groups, young people have their experiences and do their playing and talking almost wholly within a single age group. The influences do not have a vertical, in-depth dimension. The peer influences continue strong in the undergraduate years of college, and it is only later that young women realize this. For a wider perspective, it is desirable to have more discussions about your educational plans with persons of mature learning and experiences.

One difficulty in planning an academic education is that we are all blind to the possibilities that lie beyond our experiences to date. We do not know what our ultimate capabilities are and each of us has present knowledge of less than 5 percent of the occupations that may be available. (The *Dictionary of Occupational Titles* describes many tens of thousands of occupations.) We are influenced by the cultural biases of our environment, and our cultural sophistication is apt to be provincial rather than universal.

Needless to say, the kind of education you have had in high school and the quality and range of your reading and your training in art and music are important to consider when you make choices in college. A student from a disadvantaged home and community will usually be less advanced in the cultural arts and literature and in her knowledge of science than one from a home where reading is habitual and cultural interests are encouraged, and where a good school is accessible. Unfortunately, high schools vary widely in the quality of their programs, and so the graduates at the point of entrance to college are not all at the same level of achievement. This may even be true of the students graduating from the same school. Students from a good high school, as shown in one test conducted by the University of Michigan, were found to vary among themselves by eight grade levels in their achievement. In general, you have to start from where you are and then build upon that foundation.

Another way to test yourself to discover what you want to be, and hence what you should study, is to try some activities or jobs that appeal to you. This is also a good way to search for a role that is special for you as distinguished from merely doing what others do.

The experience will assist you in making a choice. Let's discuss educational theory for a moment. You know that if as a child you brushed your hand against a hot stove, the burn taught you a lesson that you have always remembered. When we say that education takes place only when an individual changes and grows, we mean that she must assimilate the ideas and make skills her own if they are to be meaningful to her or become a part of her life. This is much the same thing as to say that she must experience the education. The experiences must be educative, educative in a positive way. Some experiences can be miseducative—they may lead to antisocial behavior. Other experiences can be repetitive and routine, and hence not valuable. One therefore needs to work out a plan of action based upon objectives for educational growth—objectives of the kind discussed in Chapters 5 and 20. Experience as education is not a new idea. John Dewey wrote the best statement of the theory in his book, *Experience and Education* (New York: Macmillan, 1950).

A problem-solving type of curriculum involves the student in the scientific analysis that is required to define and solve the problems. The teacher limits her lecturing at the students to the minimum needed for orientation and interpretations, or to introduce findings from relevant research; and the student becomes involved in her own learning to a maximum degree. This learning is highly effective.

A number of colleges, including community colleges, now use the cooperative plan of work-study because it relates experience to study. The plan involves placement of the student on selected jobs, chosen for their educational value, for periods that alternate with similar periods of study at the college.

Many liberal arts colleges vary their calendars by having one month during which individualized studies and experiences may be planned. Many colleges have study-abroad programs. Some professional schools now require a clinical type of experience—law schools, for example, have introduced plans to have the students serve as legal assistants in neighborhood clinics. A few law schools do this with the deliberate attempt to reorient their graduates toward serving the needs of people instead of flocking to the big corporations.

Some extraclass activities can also be helpful in defining your goals. The most obvious case is working on the campus newspaper where a substantial training in journalism is to be had. Running for office on campus can prepare you for running for any office. A campus community needs to be governed; participation in government teaches much about governance.

In your search for what you want to study, you will benefit from talking with a college counselor. On most college campuses counselors have been chosen with great care. A complete list cannot be given for any one campus, but academic, vocational, preprofessional, psychological, psychiatric, physical, medical, and religious counseling, to mention some common ones, are available. There may also be a financial aids counselor to help you determine what benefits you may be eligible for. In most cases, a counselor, just like a physician, will help you analyze your problems; and also will direct you to a specialist if you need one.

I Wish I Had Taken It In College

HE college curriculum is packed with courses that bring before the student most of the sophisticated knowledge that exists. Although much of your program will be composed of requirements—in general education and to fulfill a major—you will nevertheless have a number of options. Some of these courses will be available to you later in life through adult and continuing education programs, but many will not be. The college years are precious in that the electives are available then. They present a golden opportunity to get experiences that result in a more meaningful education; educational experiences that will last a lifetime.

The general education requirements will probably be distributed among various broad areas of knowledge. This is to your advantage because it guides you into several cultural subjects and gives you some knowledge in each. But within each area—English, humanities, social sciences, the natural sciences—you may have considerable choice in planning your own program of studies.

The colleges have recently become more permissive in course selection than formerly. Whether for general education purposes, or to satisfy your own interests and curiosity you will have available to you a wide assortment of possible courses. A few illustrations of intriguing titles taken from actual catalogs will be suggestive of the many and varied possibilities: the Image of Women in Western Civilization, the Econom-

ics of War and Peace, the Common and Differential Characteristics of
Human Beings, Contemporary Drama, Black History, the Study of
World Culture, Political Power and Conflict, Women in Literature,
Short Story Writing, Poetry and Surrealism, Astronomy, the Psychology
of Women, Technology and Civilization, the Conservation of Natural
Resources, Basic Design, Nature Study, Mathematics for Modern Life,
Invitation to Philosophy.

Some course titles may turn you off, but nevertheless deal with subject
matter that might have meaning for you in later life. College courses can
enlarge your appreciations and contribute to making you an interesting
person. Appreciation of Music, for example, might lead to greater enjoyment of both classical and modern music; Landmarks of Literature
would probably help you to be discriminating in your reading during the
rest of your life; Introduction to Archaeology would give you perspective
on man's origin and development; History of Science might portray the
scientific method, the perfection of which has underlain the rapid advance in technology.

You may uncover these and other possibilities by searching the college
catalog—not only for titles that appeal to you, but by reading the course
descriptions carefully. Some courses may seem traditional in content, but
they may be planned to enable you to learn the best of music, art, short
stories; or how to weave, play golf, and so forth. When you are considering a course, interview the teacher, get the outline or syllabus, and find
out what the students think who have taken the course. When taking
elective courses it is not possible to cover a large amount of ground,
but one good course in art appreciation, or in conservation, or in the
theory of evolution will add a dimension to your knowledge and your
thinking.

How can you best use the opportunity to choose from among the
possible elective courses? One way is to analyze your interests as they
relate to the various facets of your life: hobbies and recreation, family
living, personal development, social orientation, and exploring for a
career. Although choosing a career will be discussed in Chapters 6 to 8,
later in this chapter we shall discuss the opportunity that some colleges
give you to seek a unique career by planning an individualized course of
study to prepare for it.

College is a period in which you can plan for leisure-time interests that
will be enjoyable in later life. The college years are formative ones.
During them you can develop interests and skills that will have a lasting

effect. After age thirty, and especially after fifty, a person becomes much more conscious of the value of avocations. They are a release from the intensity and sometimes the monotony of a job; they can be an avenue through which to weld a family together, increasing the group fun and rapport; they promote good physical health and mental attitudes. In life, we can take the activities that are thrust upon us—television, for example—or we can create some of our own. It would seem logical to learn how to select and create those activities of optimum value for happy living. It can be a frustrating experience, and sometimes a catastrophe, to meet the day when suddenly the last child has left the home, or retirement from a job has come, and the new freedom becomes a vacuum of idleness and boredom.

The college experience can include attention to hobby development. The opportunities are varied and include both formal courses and informal activities. For example, the art laboratories offer choices in creative skills; the physical education department has a rich selection of sports, both individual and group; in the departments that teach landscape architecture, horticulture, or botany are apt to be found courses that prepare you to create your own home environment and experience the pleasures of gardening; and every campus has boundless possibilities for the cultivation of civic interests.

Would you like to be better acquainted with modern painting? the psychology of personality? the dance? theater? Chinese art? the social theories of Marxists? the geological ages? You may find just what you want in the catalog; if not, you may be able to design a course of study for yourself.

Then there are courses that will acquaint you with the ideas and works of the great artists, poets, historians, scientists, philosophers. Or if you don't find the course you want, you may read independently. Picasso's paintings are doubtless known to you, but do you understand his techniques and interpretations of life? If poetry has an appeal to you, you might like to know well the works of at least one poet, T. S. Eliot or some other. Toynbee is one historian who has attempted to synthesize the events of history wherever they may have occurred, in contrast with the piecemeal examination given to those events by most historians. Thus he can give you a comprehensive view of human events and progress. Einstein provided the formula that unlocked the power in the atom. Do you feel challenged by his theory of relativity? The most indigenous philosophy in America, pragmatism, was given its initial thrust by William

James. John Dewey then used pragmatism as a basis for his theories about the best way to educate children. To understand much of what the schools do for children, it is well to understand James and Dewey.

There are many other great thinkers and doers that one might equally mention: Sigmund and Anna Freud in psychology, Keynes in economics, Dostoevski for his novels, Mozart, the great composer, Marie Curie, the Nobel Prize winner, for her work in radium, Bertrand Russell, the mathematician and philosopher, Darwin for his discovery of the evolution of life. To these few names of distinguished women and men can be added a hundred or more others who have had an unusual impact upon our beliefs and the way we live. To come to know them intimately is a rare privilege; and their writings, their art, their music facilitate this acquaintance. To know them is to help you grow in their image.

Especially significant for present-day women are the courses offered in women's studies. They attempt to correct traditional knowledge about women and their lives. They give information not offered in the regular courses which are reflections of masculine viewpoints and masculine superiority. One of their objectives is to help women to understand feminine socialization and what it has wrought over the centuries. For example, how have women been pictured in history and literature? In their research studies, do scientists include women on an equal basis with men? You might be interested to know that in making up aptitude tests, items are deleted on which women score high and men low. Women's courses explain the nature of women and are quite different from courses for women about child care and home management. With this knowledge, women can grow in self-esteem, confidence, and in achieving a sense of identity and worth.

If you are black, or interested in the white-black social problem, you might look into the new black studies courses (or for similar reasons, the Chicano or other ethnic studies) now being offered in many colleges. These courses have developed because of the demands from black students to learn about their own heritage; also because the colleges have recognized that white elitist-oriented culture is not sufficient for all students in the United States. If we are to resolve the problems of intercultural tensions, we—all of us, white, black, brown, yellow—must educate ourselves in a manner to derive common understanding and values from our pluralistic heritages. Hence the colleges have begun to offer courses in the various ethnic areas—for example, the history, art, literature, psychology, and sociology of black people. If you are white, you need some of this knowledge in order to emancipate yourself from prejudices and to help free American society from its demeaning attitudes toward people who differ in their skin pigments and their heritage. Through these additions, the college is departing from its Western-oriented bias in favor of ethnic studies derived from various cultures resident in America.

If you are greatly troubled by the image that America seems to be getting in the world, and concerned about the methods we have been using in establishing cultural and trade relations with other peoples, one thing you can do in college is to inform yourself about these questions and their backgrounds. At the least, you can find ways in which to get more accurate information than you've had and broaden your views about people of other cultures. We have been taught that white, Western culture is superior to others, that the Christian religion is infallible, and that our economic individualism and enterprise is the best system. Are these beliefs wholly sound?

It is also mere common sense to search for wisdom wherever you may find it. Others than Americans have some of it. Assuming all religions share in presenting good ethics and philosophy, it is important in becoming well educated to uncover the values that are portrayed in the several religious creeds and synthesize them for your own use. You may wish to learn to appreciate the classical symphonies, but do not overlook the music that Asians enjoy equally well. Come to know the cultural histories of China and India, which predate ours by many centuries, with resulting accumulations of art, literature and wisdom. We of the West should know them better, for their own values and to gain fresh insights. For purposes such as the above, you will discover special courses such as Oriental Art, Chinese History, or Comparative Religions.

Another meaningful experience in gaining intercultural knowledge would be to enroll in a study-abroad program offered by many colleges. If you take advantage of study in a foreign country for a semester or a year, you can gain an in-depth experience with the language, literature, politics, geography, and many other things. You would live in the culture while studying it, an obvious advantage.

If you marry, you may be living some if not all of your post-college years with a man, just as a male student has the expectation of living with a woman. How can the college experience contribute toward successes in the woman-man relationship? What courses are offered with this in view? There are courses that you and your husband-to-be might take together: Human Sexuality, Child Development, The Social History of Women, Gourmet Styles, and Consumer Economics are examples. Other possible selections will be found in such departments as psychology, sociology, and physical education.

In short, elective courses offer you ways you can enhance your personal interests, help you to become a person of culture, and deepen your appreciations of fine things. Since each person is a unique individual, your interests may not conform to those of other students. You should be aware that many colleges will permit you to plan a course for yourself that differs from those described by the departments of the college. Through this plan, you may choose a subject of special interest to you—for example, Japanese drama, or the liberation of women, or foods chemistry. In working out your plan of study you will learn a lot about how to learn, that is, how to plan an investigation, identify a problem, collect information, study applicable theories and techniques, and write about the findings. Thus the experience pays double dividends—an interesting subject matter, and increased skills in learning.

It may also be possible to do group study. A selected problem, for example, might be examined by three or four students, each using a special approach. Then they would prepare a paper on the subject. A study of the commune movement, for example, would have psychological, sociological, economic, and historical facets, so a student from each of those areas might participate. Or a study of poverty in a ghetto could best be done by a group having similar interdisciplinary skills. This is one way to jump the departmental walls in a college and bring interdisciplinary concepts and tools together.

Some colleges will permit you to go beyond one or two individualized courses by helping you to arrange an individual field of concentration. This means planning your own major study, rather than merely following the requirements for a departmental major. Nearly all colleges are organized by departments—English, mathematics, sociology, biology, and so forth. It is a convenience in administration to plan the majors for study in relation to these departments. Such majors serve the purposes of most students because they have not thought beyond the possibility of becoming a psychologist, an economist, or a physicist. However, there are reasons why this neat arrangement does not always work best for the education of the student. For one thing, she may be sufficiently inventive to visualize a career for herself that does not fit the stereotyped pattern; or, she may define a problem or area of study for which an interdisciplinary approach is needed; or, she may want to study in a broad area such as the social sciences rather than in only one of them. As an example of an individual field major, you might arrange one on the conservation and management of natural resources. For this major, you could combine selected courses from biology, physical geography, economics, and political science, together with certain studies that you plan on your own.

The answer to your need lies in persuading the college that you are capable of planning your own major study and of defining the educational outcomes that you propose to achieve. The college in turn will define what constitutes an in-depth study sufficient to satisfy the requirements for a degree. A professor can then be chosen to counsel you in planning your studies and later to evaluate your achievement.

All that has been said above is about possible actions that require your initiative. Colleges and universities offer an amazing variety of courses and educational experiences. Now is the time to explore them. Four years, two years from now may be too late. Ten years from now you will be saying, "I wish I had taken it in college."

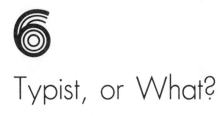

Typist, or What?

HE image that we have of the woman graduate, diploma in hand after four years of study, being shunted into a position as typist is all too realistic. But the career-motivated woman, with a little searching, will find that the opportunities for women are almost as diverse as for men. To take advantage of them, however, requires an examination of your own talents and interests, information about the job possibilities, and some imaginative planning while in college.

Do you like research? Women are as qualified for research—whether in the natural or social sciences, or in historiography—as are men. One needs, of course, the basic tools and some knowledge relating to the particular discipline—chemistry, mathematics, sociology, archeology, or whatever is chosen. Some areas of research may seem to be crowded, but there is always room for a person who is resourceful and competent. A research career is for those who are challenged by problem solving and discovery. However, for every original investigator, there are many members of the technical staffs.

Are you interested in the care and study of animals—pets, or horses, for example? Are you concerned about the conditions under which milk and meats are produced? If so, you may find the practice of veterinary medicine a rewarding experience. It is also a profession that can be conducted from one's home. The image of the veterinarian as a man dates from the days when he had to slosh through the dung on the floor of the cow barns. Dairy barns are now sanitized; pets are brought to the vet's own hospital. Animals can be tranquilized rather than having to be hog-tied when being treated.

If you like languages, why not become proficient in one where personnel are scarce, where modern literature is growing, or where the needs for foreign personnel are pressing? Possibilities include Chinese, Russian, Japanese, Swahili, Hindi, or perhaps other languages that are relatively unfamiliar to Americans.

If you are interested in the causes of racism or other intercultural problems, consider anthropology. Cultural anthropology is an especially good foundation for foreign service, and is useful in various fields of social service where intercultural differences, such as skin pigment, may be basic to the poverty or disadvantaged environment that prevails. Field investigations can lead to valuable discoveries as Mary Leakey and her late husband, Louis, both anthropologists, have proved in Africa. They have extended the age of man from perhaps 100,000 years to a few million; and they have posed the hypothesis that Africa was the original home of the human race. Jane Van Lawick-Goodall has illuminated man's beginnings through her research in Africa by proving that chimpanzees make tools for use in getting food. Perhaps man learned to use tools in the same manner.

Are you good at figures? Women who are trained as accountants are being extensively used by the Internal Revenue Service to counsel people about their tax problems, and to audit the returns. Accounting, a field needing personnel, opens many doors to opportunity in business, in government, and as a public accountant.

With the invention of the computer whole new fields of employment have opened for women who have aptitude for mathematics. The principal ones are as programmers for the computer, and as data processors. They require some knowledge of the fundamentals of statistics and some skills that are not too difficult to learn. If your throat gets dry at the thought of statistics, just take a swallow and go on. It is nonsense to say that since you are a woman you cannot acquire competence in statistical methods. The point is that here is an expanding field of employment that opens doors to governmental services, research, management, factory systems, information services, and countless other interesting and colorful opportunities.

While women should not be limited to office work, and a job as secretary may be routine, it can nevertheless lead to an interesting career.

Whether you remain a typist or file clerk, or use these jobs as a stepping stone, depends upon how much responsibility you can or are willing to assume. There is no shortage of persons who can do routine clerical tasks, but there is a good demand for persons who can become supervisors, office managers, and secretaries to executives. A competent secretary becomes almost indispensable when she learns how to manage the executive's appointments, correspondence, and travel. Sometimes on important questions that come before the executive, the decisions are actually made by the secretary. The secretarial supervisory position occasionally leads to a high administrative role, even as chief executive.

A woman is as competent to be an architect as a man. She might be even more insightful as a designer and skillful as a draftswoman. Landscape architecture is a "natural" for the woman who enjoys nature and prefers to work for specific clients and on a part-time basis. The new surge of interest by the schools of architecture (or environmental design) for the study of environment should attract women as students.

Department stores employ women in large numbers. Some of them prefer college women as sales personnel, and this may be a good entrance for one who thinks of retailing as a career. But the larger stores present many opportunities as buyers, personnel officers, and staff in advertising. One of the largest stores in New York has a woman as president as do several other nationally known retail companies. Merit counts for more than sex in large-scale retailing, especially in fields where women predominate as the shoppers.

Women who major in English often say that they have difficulty in finding positions other than in teaching. This is due in considerable part to lack of knowledge about the possibilities that are open. The publishing field uses women, probably more women than men, as editors and as research writers. Newspapers and magazines use women as reporters, researchers, writers, and editors. TV and radio stations have women script writers, announcers, and program directors. Museums require writers for educational materials. Any enterprise that publicizes its products or services must have people who can write.

Labor organizations employ large technical staffs to produce educational materials and to compile economic data. The labor movement has reached a stage of maturity where success is determined by skills at the bargaining table. The negotiators also must have competent staff to supply them with research data, carefully reasoned analyses of the issues at stake, and position papers for influencing the decisions. Women, as well as men, are needed for all these important roles.

Are you concerned about people, the environment in which they live and work, their poverty, health, family planning, drug addiction, and other problems? If so, you might serve their needs by becoming a social worker or health specialist.

There are literally hundreds of other career opportunities for which the colleges—although not every college—offer preparation.

Would you like to know what other young women of your age generally think about potential careers? The SCOPE survey (Chapter 4) asked the opinions of several thousand women now in college. Among fifteen possible roles from which they were asked to choose the ones at which they thought they would be good, the women named teacher, confidant, and creator at the top of the list. They also showed preference for the roles of organizer, competitor, and protector. The majority did not see themselves as healer, politician, pioneer, beachcomber, law-enforcer, or research scholar. They liked somewhat each of the remaining three roles of arbitrator, critic, and promoter.

When the undergraduate women in the Carnegie study (Chapter 4) were asked to choose between service roles and administrative ones, they selected the former. Since nearly all of these women said that they planned to marry and have a home, probably they perceived administrative jobs as placing too many demands upon their time and energies. However, one-fourth of them said they would accept a role as an administrator. But the choice of service occupations is good, because those occupations have shown steady growth in the demand for college-educated personnel.

Such a list of broad, functional roles gives you one perspective from which to think about careers. If you can identify your interests and talents in reference to the functional kind of work that most appeals to you, you will have made a good beginning in searching for a particular career.For example, the role of competitor might lead you into business; an organizer would find a good place in politics, a teacher would be employed in a school; and so forth.

The freshman women in the ACE study (Chapter 4) were asked to identify their potential career, based upon a list of occupations that are usual to college graduates. The female-oriented occupations—teacher, health professional, nurse, and artist—ranked the highest. The full results for the survey made in 1972 are shown in table 2. The "other" category included a wide scattering of possible careers, such as account-

2. CAREER CHOICES OF FRESHMAN WOMEN

Career	Percent
Elementary teacher	11.1%
Educator (secondary)	8.4
Health professional (non M.D.)	10.4
Nurse	9.8
Artist (including performer)	8.0
Businesswoman	4.8
Doctor (M.D. or D.D.S.)	2.8
Research scientist	1.5
Lawyer	2.0
Farmer or forester	.7
College teacher	.6
Engineer	.3
Clergywoman	.2
Other	24.9
Undecided	14.4
Total	**99.9%**

Source: American Council on Education (ACE) survey, 1971.

3. PROSPECTIVE EMPLOYERS OF COLLEGE WOMEN

Employer	Percent
Elementary or secondary school system	20.7%
Self-employed professional practice	9.5
Hospital or clinic	7.3
Research organization or institute	6.7
Business or industry	6.0
Self-employed or family business	5.2
College or university	4.5
Other non-profit organization (church, welfare agency)	4.5
Federal government	4.0
Partner or associate in professional practice	4.2
State or local government	1.8
Junior college	.7
Other	7.5
Not answered	17.3
Total	**99.9%**

Source: Carnegie Commission on Higher Education, 1969–70.

4. EMPLOYED PERSONS, BY MAJOR OCCUPATION AND SEX, 1950, 1960, 1972

IN THOUSANDS OF PERSONS

	1950		1960		1972	
	Female	*Male*	*Female*	*Male*	*Female*	*Male*
White-collar workers	8824	13549	12129	16596	18832	20059
Professional/Technical	1794	2696	2706	4768	4614	6969
Managers, Officials, Proprietors	990	5439	1099	5967	1303	6507
Clerical	4597	3035	6629	3154	10722	3468
Sales	1443	2379	1695	2707	2194	3114
Blue-collar workers	3608	19727	3637	20573	4569	23175
Service	3850	2685	5431	2918	6877	4189
Farm	1212	6196	998	4398	501	2425

Source: *Statistical Abstract of the U.S. 1972*, p. 230, table 366.

ant, architect, computer programmer, foreign service worker, interior designer, musician, optometrist, statistician, veterinarian, and so forth.

In the Carnegie study, which included upperclass women, the women were asked to state the type of employer they would prefer. Their choices are shown in table 3.

On the whole, the preferences stated in the two studies are similar. In both of them, teaching is the top choice. This may soon change, however, since at present there is a marked oversupply of teachers. When upperclass women, as well as freshmen, were included, teaching in college became a more important choice—this is an example of the increased awareness you acquire as you progress through college. The number selecting the junior college, however, is small; the high potential in this work is being overlooked. Junior or community colleges not only give more employment to women relative to men than do senior colleges, but they also have highly interesting programs and are growing rapidly in enrollments. Nineteen percent of the undergraduate women expressed preference for some kind of self-employment or professional practice that resembles self-employment.

What are the trends in the employment of women? What kinds of jobs do women in general have? The number of women employed in 1970 compared with the number in 1960 showed a large increase. A projection for 1980 made by the U.S. Government shows a continuing increase. This is evidence of growing opportunities, but also of greater competition for jobs. Since 1948 the percent of mothers who work has steadily increased about one percent a year. Approximately 80 percent of college women go to work immediately following their graduation. Women who get advanced degrees work in even larger numbers. Ninety-one percent of women with doctorates are employed, or self-employed, 81 percent of them full time.

Table 4 shows the number of employed persons by major occupation and by sex in the years 1950, 1960, and 1972. Among the white-collar workers, women outnumbered the men only in the clerical category; men predominated in the professional and technical fields and among managers and proprietors. But in all broad fields, the number of women employed is large.

Some women do not work a full week. In the category of professional and technical workers, for example, 50.5 percent of the women worked 50 to 52 hours per week; 13.7 percent worked 27 to 49 hours; and 12.4 percent worked 26 or less hours. The remainder worked in jobs that were defined as part-time.

Two-fifths of the wives of professional and technical workers were in the same major occupation as their husbands. But among jobs of all kinds only one-fifth of the married couples pursued similar employment.

A college education normally leads to employment in a profession or a technical field. Table 5 shows by sub-categories the number of women in these types of work.

Women may find employment in business, industry, various institutions, and the professions. They also find good opportunity in governmental service. The federal government in 1970 had 714,000 women in its employ, and in a tremendous variety of positions. This was 27 percent of the total for women and men, and compared with 25 percent in 1960 and 24 percent in 1950. The increase in the employment of women is encouraging, but the rate of growth is less than the times warrant. Slightly more than three-fourths of the positions in the government are white-collar.

Although the ratios of women to men in the data given above vary widely, some women—and not in trifling numbers—engage in almost every calling as do men, at least in those for which a college education is a requisite. In choosing an occupation for yourself, you may prefer to enter one into which women go in large numbers. But on the other hand, you should also consider the kinds of work into which fewer women have ventured. As noted in Chapter 8, the male-dominated fields of law, medicine, dentistry, architecture, engineering, and college teaching are

5. WOMEN AS PROFESSIONAL AND TECHNICAL WORKERS, 1970

Occupation	Number of women (in thousands)	Percent of all persons in occupation
Accountants	187.0	26.2%
Architects	2.0	3.6
Engineers	20.3	1.6
Farm and Home Management Advisers	6.5	49.7
Lawyers and Judges	13.4	4.9
Librarians	101.5	82.0
Life and Physical Scientists	29.2	13.7
Personnel and Labor Relations Workers	91.7	30.9
Pharmacists	13.3	12.0
Physicians, Medical and Osteopathic	26.1	9.3
Dietitians	37.8	92.0
Registered Nurses	819.3	97.3
Therapists	48.5	63.5
Health Technicians	184.1	69.7
Clergywomen	6.3	2.9
Other Religious Workers	20.1	55.7
Social Scientists	32.0	23.2
Social Workers	138.9	62.8
Recreation Workers	22.5	42.0
Teachers, Elementary	1199.4	83.7
Teachers, Secondary	498.7	49.3
Teachers, College and University	140.4	28.6
Engineering and Science Technicians	68.7	12.9
Draftswomen	23.6	8.0
Radio Operators	7.6	25.9
Authors	7.7	29.1
Dancers	5.7	81.3
Designers	27.2	24.2
Editors and Reporters	61.5	40.6
Musicians and Composers	33.5	34.8
Photographers	9.5	14.2
Other Professional, Technical, and Kindred Workers	513.9	32.9

Source: Economic Report of the President, January 1973, p. 155, table 33.

now opening to women in larger numbers. Other possibilities include industrial management, veterinary medicine, work with senior citizens, urban planning, banking, brokerage, and financial institutions. If you like to do things with your hands, you might consider work as a technician or repairperson. Repairs to appliances, automobiles and scientific equipment are now being made with replacement parts, rather than being overhauled as formerly, and so the need is for persons with manual dexterity and knowledge of blueprints and use of sophisticated instruments rather than muscle power. The electrical and telephone industries are opening more of the technician types of job to women.

If you can't decide what kind of career most appeals to you, or if you have started on something and then find that you dislike it, you are not trapped. There are steps you can take to clarify your thinking and to change. Janice, one of the students interviewed in depth by the authors, was studying art at a private college specializing in fine and applied arts. Although she liked art and did well in her studies, she had chosen this field because of pressure from her mother. Her parents had achieved middle-class status through education and hard work, and her mother held a position as a librarian. They were naturally desirous of seeing their daughter educated for a good position. As a future teacher of art, Janice—a black woman—would find employment and have security.

But Janice became unhappy with her choice of vocation. The reason was that she had spent a summer vacation working in a medical laboratory and she had liked this work; indeed had been much stimulated by it. She kept thinking about this experience, and now she wondered why she had not studied for a medical career. But being a woman, and also black, she was torn by the uncertainty of getting into medical school and later having an opportunity to practice medicine. Also, she reasoned, it would be unfair to ask her parents to finance her for a long, expensive period if the end result was only frustration. At this point she consulted with a counselor who was knowledgeable about various vocational opportunities. She was able to give Janice information about the urgent need for more physicians, about the special need for more black physicians, including women, about recent actions by the medical schools in admitting many more women, and about the scholarships and loans that are available to medical students. With this additional knowledge in hand, Janice decided to transfer to a premedical course of study.

Thus Janice, by the end of her first year in college, had taken three steps to define her goals: she had had an intensive experience in a job she liked, she had tried certain college courses, and she had sought professional advice. There are still other steps you can take. For example, you can analyze carefully what you would like to do in life. It is not easy to do in advance, because the possibilities for a career extend much beyond the ones that are obvious to you from the limited experiences you have had by college age. There are literally thousands of possibilities from among which you may choose.

A college has tests to use in self-analysis, including some that will clarify your vocational interests. When you have answered the questions on the instrument, and interpreted the significance of your answers, you will be better able to select the courses in which you should enroll. The self-analysis includes tests of aptitudes. Some people possess unusual manual dexterity, some are especially good at spatial recognition, some have personal handicaps, and some possess intelligence that is different in type from others. There are tests that can help you decide what your best personal resources are, and what deficiencies might limit your choice of occupation. There is also much literature on the subject. A counselor can assist you to get such materials and take appropriate tests. Vocational counselors in college are trained, experienced, and willing to help you.

You can approach with an open mind the courses that are required of you as part of your general education. These courses are intended to offer you samples of various fields of study as a means of acquainting you with new interests, vocational as well as cultural, with which you may not have had previous contact. Even if these courses seem to you to be superficial, use their outlines to discover fresh interests and as guides for deeper study on your own. Make a tentative choice and then try it.

As implied throughout this discussion, a woman student must face the question of her own attitudes about a career. One study of high school graduates showed that high percentages of women felt they did not have the ability to undertake certain professions. For example, 57 percent of them felt that they could not qualify to become a lawyer, 66 percent a research scientist, 70 percent a physician, and 86 percent an engineer. Another survey showed that women perceived themselves as intellectuals less often than did men students. (Yet girls do consistently better academic work in high school than do boys.) Women do succeed well as lawyers, scientists, physicians, and engineers. The presumption is that young women at the high school age have been conditioned by opinions, often repeated in the home, at church, and in the community, to think that because they are women they have less aptitude for certain occupations than do men. Attitudes such as these have been pressed upon a woman from early childhood—for example, that she should avoid a male-oriented occupation, or that she should select something that requires a feminine touch, or that maintains her feminine image. If as a college student you yield to these feelings, you will find yourself fettered by tradition.

The trend in women's thinking about their lives is in the opposite direction. They want to live a full life, a rounded life. This includes for many having a career. By the time you will have become launched in a career, a career will have become the expected thing for a college-educated woman.

7

A Career with a Future

WHEN searching for a career for yourself it is especially important to try to find one that will have a good future. Often this means avoiding fields that are popular at the moment because they may become overcrowded. What careers for women will be best ten, twenty or more years after you leave college? You should anticipate that there will be social changes that will influence the employment opportunities of the future and consider what type of work would continue to be productive, creative, and challenging to you thirty years hence. What fields of effort are now on the threshold of expansion? Is it possible that some kind of self-employment will best meet your expectations?

The Women's Bureau of the U.S. Department of Labor has estimated that the growth rate for various broad categories of employment between 1970 and 1980 will be as follows: professional and technical workers, 39 percent; service workers, 35 percent; clerical workers, 26 percent; sales workers, 24 percent; craftsmen and foremen, 20 percent; managers and administrators, 15 percent; and operatives, 11 percent. To demonstrate how to identify careers that have future growth potential, we shall describe three professional and technical areas briefly—health services, ecology, and the technical staffs of business and the professions.

Health is a factor in the life of every person. Hence the health needs in a nation grow with growth in population, and they also increase as the standard of living increases and as the attention to health shifts from the treatment of disease to keeping people well. In the United States great advances have been made in conquering disease. This is the result of the enormous attention that has been given to scientific research by the medical profession and by the agencies, governmental and otherwise, that provide the funds. Doubtless the research will be continued and will provide many highly satisfying opportunities for employment and service.

It is a strange anomaly, however, that with the advances of research and specialization among the practitioners, the health services to many segments of the population have deteriorated. Infant mortality, for example, in the United States is much higher than in several other nations in the world. Moreover, within the country the discrepancies in the rates of mortality among various socioeconomic groups are scandalous—infant mortality among blacks is approximately twice that for whites. These results can be attributed directly to the bias of medical faculties toward research, the admission to medical school of elite personnel with primary interests in science, and the growth of specializations in medical practice. Affluent persons get good medical services; other people often do not. It seems clear that a reorganization of medical services is needed and will occur. The future stress will be upon the patient, and ways will be found to make the health services more readily available to all. It seems probable that a national health services program of some kind will be instituted.

With this change, the opportunities for women should open wide. The contention that women are not productive in science—false though it may be—would no longer be a reason for discriminating against them as physicians. Women have good aptitudes for patient care, a factor as valid for using them as physicians as for nurses. A shift from entrepreneurial medicine, which we now have, in favor of a health services program, means group practice and teamwork. In a study of preference for professional practice, 43 percent of the women preferred employed practice, whereas only 11 percent of the men did. Women make good members of the team. Also, to provide adequate services a large increase in the number of doctors, medical assistants and nurses will be required. Health service is said to be our third largest industry. It may become the largest one.

Although women should aspire to be physicians, dentists, and nurses, they have many additional choices. The U.S. Department of Health, Education, and Welfare lists three hundred occupations in the health field. Of these, about one hundred require one or more years of college. They represent a tremendous variety of interests and requirements in education. The following are given merely to illustrate the composition of the list: biochemist, corrective therapist, dental hygienist, food and drug inspector, medical illustrator, medical librarian, medical technologist, optometrist, orthoptist, pharmacist, physician, psychiatric social worker, psychometrist, public health educator, radiological health specialist, sanitarian, speech pathologist and audiologist, vocational rehabilitation counselor.*

A new development of great potential interest to women is the opening of career ladders for nurses. The medical and nursing schools at the University of Colorado are training Nurse Pediatrics Practitioners (and a few other universities are following suit). These are nurses with advanced training that includes partial preparation as physicians. It is estimated that as practitioners they will be able to do about 80 percent of the work of examining and caring for well babies. This is the opening wedge for a new level of general practitioner to supplement the physician. It is feasible not only in pediatrics, but also in a number of other medical specializations.

What are the possibilities in ecology, another field of potential growth in the future? College students have been in the vanguard in alerting people and the government to the wastage of our natural resources and the pollution of the air and water. As a consequence of growing national concern, it is highly probable that the requirements for personnel in conservation, in clearing up pollution, and in the other aspects of ecology, will be expanded severalfold. Doubtless many college-educated women will find in this urgent situation a challenge for their life's work.

Columnist Sylvia Porter has estimated the near-future needs, shown in table 6. She did not differentiate the workers by sex, but all of the occupations listed would include women.

The possibilities for working to improve our environment also go considerably beyond the efforts in conservation. Among the needs are the following:

---

*For more complete information consult publications of the U.S. Department of Health, Education and Welfare, *Health Manpower Source Book;* U.S. Department of Labor, *Health Careers Guidebook;* and American Medical Women's Association, *Career Choices for Women in Medicine,* vols. 1 and 2.

	6. WORKERS IN KEY FIELDS (ESTIMATES)	
Field	Workers 1971	Needed 1980
Ecology	4,300	12,000
Geology	22,800	33,400
Geophysics	6,800	10,400
Meteorology	4,000	12,000
Oceanography	5,800	40,000
Forestry	24,000	37,000
Forestry aids	13,000	23,800
Range management	6,000	8,000
Soil conservation	26,000	30,000
Wildlife conservation	15,000	20,000
Fisheries conservation	4,500	7,500
Recreation and parks	215,790	220,000
Architecture	34,000	61,600
Engineering (construction)	40,000	70,000
Landscape architecture	8,500	14,500
Urban planning	7,000	16,600
Environmental protection	217,500	565,000

Source: Sylvia Porter, "Future Careers in Conservation," *San Francisco Chronicle,* September 23, 1971, p. 30.

Environmental psychology: a sparsely populated field, concerned with what one observer calls "the crisis in human dignity" in the face of environmental degradation.

Environmental education: teaching about a wide range of building and restoring structures, neighborhoods, towns and outdoor spaces, covering specialties from city planning to landscape architecture.

Environmental geology: investigation of immediate and long-term environmental needs; sedimentation in lakes, waste disposal.

Water hygiene: study of chemical as well as bacteriological contamination of water supplies aimed at protecting consumers.

Radiological health: control of dangerous levels of radiation, from such devices as microwave ovens and atomic power plants.

Community environmental management: exploring solutions to the effects of such poverty conditions as overcrowding, rats, noise and air pollution, on the 15 percent who live in their midst.

Colleges and universities provide fields of study in the area of ecology. Several of them are named in table 6. There are others, including anthropology, physics, entomology, biology, desert research, agricultural climatology, agricultural engineering, botany, arctic biology, biometrics, watershed management, population problems, earth sciences, range science, plant pathology, aquatic biology, agronomy, medical mycology, limnology, hydrology, genetics, and alpine research.*

The third illustrative type of employment with a future is as technician or subprofessional. Some of these positions may be familiar to you: for example, dental hygienist, laboratory analyst, bookkeeper, draftswoman, and so forth. But there are literally hundreds of technical specializations in business, engineering and the professions. This career field has been growing rapidly and steadily. The reasons lie in the manner in which work that requires technical training can be subdivided when professional people work together in firms or clinical groups, when services become institutionalized as in hospitals, and when business enterprise and the divisions of government become larger and more complex.

Our technologically based society has been steadily displacing the manual laborer, but at the same time it has been creating roles for skilled personnel. This category of employee is becoming the largest of any in the labor market. Here are some training programs which community colleges offer: fashion arts, graphic arts, aircraft flight operations, business equipment technology, electrical control technology, electronic communication technology, photography, cosmetology, quality control, culinary arts, and dental assisting. This list can be expanded materially. The best way to become acquainted with the variety of programs that exist is to get the catalogs of several public community colleges, and also the descriptions of the programs in medical, dental, nursing, engineering, business, and other schools, because many of the professional schools have programs for training paraprofessional personnel.**

One other possibility for you to consider is self-employment. Because of the need for capital and the severity of competition, self-employment is not easy at the start, but it has distinct appeal. If successful, you will have achieved independence of action and greater control over your life. Many young women and men choose arts and crafts as their field of

---

*For a more complete discussion of this expanding field, see Odom Fanning, *Opportunities in Environmental Careers* (New York: Universal Publishing and Distributing Corporation, 1972).

**For further information, see Norman C. Harris, *Developments in Technical and Vocational Education* (Washington, D.C.: U.S. Department of Health, Education and Welfare, 1969).

interest, and make and sell their own products in bazaars, fairs, and elsewhere. This can be a creative, satisfying experience for some; but the marketing of the art objects might not produce much income for you if the field became overcrowded or if your products were not distinctive. In the national scene, urban and otherwise, the largest concentration of self-employed women is in retail trade, such as the sale of apparel and accessories, where they are proprietors. Many businesses that serve food and drinks or sell food and dairy products, or that provide personal services, are owned by women.

The opportunities to create a life of your own choosing are often more available if you live in a small community. In earlier college generations the way to "get ahead" was to go to an urban center and get a job with a large corporation. This provided an income, security, and the excitement of living where the action was. Then came the reaction among college students against materialistic rewards and parasitic living. Is this what life is about?

Have you considered living in a small community? Life in a small community can be more modest and less competitive, the relations with other people can be on a neighborly basis, the activities and associations of growing children will be less structured and less pressured by environmental influences, and the opportunities for creative work in the community will usually be large. One of the problems of smaller communities is the total inadequacy of professional services. Many communities find ways to subsidize young practitioners, especially in the health field, while they are getting started.

A person with creative talents and administrative skills can found an enterprise of her own. The smaller community is often the best place to do this because the community needs the economic activity and the competition may be less severe. An example is found in Yellow Springs, Ohio. There various women and men initiated enterprises: a plastics factory, a nonferrous metal foundry, a laboratory for delicate instruments, a bookplate company, a processing laboratory of granite surface plates for research laboratories, a stained glass studio, two design companies, photographic studios, a processing mill of farm seeds, an advertising agency, a dog kennel, and several others. The largest company, now employing several hundred women and men, was started as an art bronze foundry in an old barn. A woman did much of the research that enabled the enterprise to grow, and she is now the president of the company.

Another possibility is to go into politics, either in a small or large community. There are about a hundred women mayors of cities in the United States. A number of women have become representatives or senators in Congress and in the state legislatures. Two of our states have had women as governors. A few women have become judges and two have become members of the President's cabinet. Looking abroad, one sees that women have been prime ministers in India, Ceylon, and Israel. There is no legal obstruction to running for public office and it seems highly probable that the number of women in policy forming, administrative, and judicial roles will rise appreciably within the next half century. We are especially in need of more women in the state legislatures, in Congress, and as judges.

Finally, the best opportunity for self-employment for you may be as a practitioner with your own office. The several professions—law, medicine, dentistry, architecture, consulting engineer or scientist, clinical psychologist—offer this possibility.

The discussions of health services, ecology, and technical staffs, and of self-employment, are merely illustrative of fields that seem to have more than ordinary possiblities for future growth. The analyses suggest ways in which you can search for a career that would have high potential for you in the future.

Career Discriminations against Women

I N choosing a career, you should be aware that as a college-educated woman you will be competing with men, especially if you aim for a job with high prestige or responsibility. Men have vested interests—they are the establishment—in professions such as law or medicine, and in the administration of business and government. Men resist moving over and letting a woman in.

The problems that Juanita, a Woodrow Wilson Fellow of 1959, met en route to a career as a college teacher are all too common. She and her boyfriend, Peter, both wanted to be college teachers and, desiring to be together, applied to the same graduate school. Juanita had a better grade-point average than did Peter, and had received a Woodrow Wilson Fellowship, a very high honor. So she was astonished when Peter was accepted and she was not. She sought the help of her departmental chairman, but he advised her not to go ahead with her plans as women were seldom employed by colleges in her chosen field. Nevertheless, she persisted and did gain admission to another graduate school.

Following their marriage, both Juanita and Peter took it for granted that her husband's career would determine where they would live and work. This limited her opportunity to the colleges in a narrow geographical area. A rule on nepotism prevented her from teaching at the same institution as her husband. The husband's job took precedence, and so she had to find a position in a lesser institution.

55

Here, she presently discovered, two other persons of her age and preparation had been employed at the same time. But the two men had received appointments as assistant professor, whereas she was given the title of instructor. One consequence was that they would be entitled to consideration for tenure and she would not be. Furthermore, she was assigned a heavier teaching load than they on the ground that a man needed some time for research. Within the department, which was skewed heavily in favor of men, she was given a lot of secretarial chores to do. At the departmental meetings, she was always asked to take the minutes. Frequently she was overlooked—indeed the men seemed to forget that she was a member of the faculty—when conferences were held to make academic decisions. She was told by one man that the place for a married woman was in the home. But she observed that the unmarried woman had similar problems, and in addition had difficulty in finding a place in the social life of the community.

Juanita's problems might become your problems. You should be aware of those fields where discrimination is greatest because it may affect your life; but you should also weigh the possibilities for change and consider the role you might play in bringing about change.

The principal source of discrimination lies in social attitudes about the role of women and about their competence to do certain types of work. The social attitudes toward women make them the victims of many informal policies and practices. Officers in employment agencies habitually steer women to learn to type well so that they can fall back upon typing as a job. Recruitment officers who visit the campuses commonly have women identified for certain categories of positions. They seek airline hostesses, bank tellers, and army-navy nurses. Within some of the occupations, the women find that they are outside of the system of informal communication—rap sessions, lunch companions, golf teams, and so forth. Thus they are not well informed about events that may affect them and are not present when the decisions are really being made. Some male employers feel that when a woman is in the laboratory or attends committee meetings, she tends to be disruptive to serious thought and discussion. This is, of course, the same old argument that for so long prevented women from attending Michigan, Harvard, Yale, and other colleges. Nepotism, as Juanita discovered, almost always eliminates the wife rather than the husband from consideration.

Laws in some states discriminate against women. Although well intended as protections for women, they serve also as barriers. For example, women cannot work at night or over eight hours in some states and this prevents them from attaining supervisory positions. Laws such as these, enacted when it was common for women to be employed in sweatshops, are less warranted now when employment conditions for both women and men are better regulated. The obsolete laws should be changed; meanwhile, young women should be aware that restrictive laws do exist and do limit women in their choices of work. It seems probable that by the time that you seek employment, the equal rights amendment to the United States Constitution will have been approved by the states and thus will have made the discriminatory laws unconstitutional.

One of the problems encountered by women students in graduate school is that the male professor prefers not to train a woman as his understudy. These professors are obsessed with the old idea that a woman cannot sustain herself in rigorous intellectual work and also that a woman in later life will not be able to give continuity to work. They rationalize their viewpoints by citing that only five women have become Nobel Prize winners (but five *have* won the prize). They also assert that women are not as productive as men in publication, but this will bear scrutiny because the men who write scholarly dissertations greatly outnumber the women who do. Some studies have demonstrated that when individuals are compared with individuals, women are as productive as men.

A study of discrimination against women as faculty made at the University of California in 1970 pinpointed the prejudices against women as graduate students: "There are departments where women students are told in seminars that women are unable to think objectively or analytically. There are departments where suggestions that women might be dissatisfied with the present state of affairs are met with jibes or with scornful comments about aggressive women."

Some professions are male-oriented, or at least male-dominated. In college teaching, women in 1972 represented about 27 percent of the faculty. This low percentage is explained in various ways. Women do not get doctor's degrees in as high numbers as men, although in 1972 women represented 37 percent of the graduate students. The belief is held that women do not pursue research with the same vigor and persistence as men. Then there are the large applied fields of agriculture, business, and engineering where the women students number few; hence those prepared for college teaching are fewer than men. Women have no difficulty in entering the female-oriented fields such as education, social work, and home economics, although many of the administrative jobs are held by men. However, most departmental chairmen in the liberal arts consider a woman only when her qualifications are definitely superior to other candidates; otherwise, the choice goes to a man.

Comparative data show that both Columbia and the University of California, Berkeley, have been large producers of doctoral degrees for women, but small employers of women on their faculties. They are institutions of high prestige—the type of institution where the discrimination against women is most evident.

Among scientists in 1968 the ratio stood 90.7 percent men and 9.3 percent women. The representation of women in certain sciences, however, is somewhat better than indicated. In chemistry it is 25, in psychology 21, in biology 17, and in mathematics 12 percent.

Among lawyers, until quite recently, about 3 percent have been women. They have been rather heavily concentrated in the areas of domestic relations and estate problems. It has been argued that women are not good in adversary situations such as prevail in the courts. This seems doubtful, but even if it were valid, so much of law today concerns business, real estate, insurance and legislation, plus the functioning of corporations and administrative agencies in government, that the adversary relationship in court becomes a lesser consideration. Law, which at heart is the regulation of human affairs and the adjustment of problems of human relations, should appeal to more women. In one study of the humanitarian motivations of students, it was found that 56.7 percent of the women, and only 30.7 percent of the men in law had strong humanitarian motivations. If more of the lawyers were women, they could help reorient the law to human needs as distinguished from corporate profits and expensive litigation. The number of women in law schools has increased almost ninefold in the past decade—from 1,883 to 16,760. In 1973 women made up 15.6 percent of the enrollment.

Engineering is a profession that has been much dominated by men, women making up about one percent of the total. This is a holdover from the day when men were the surveyors, bridge builders, and oil and mineral developers. But engineering is changing, and with the change, the field, or rather the many fields, may become more appealing to women for careers. Engineering is now going beyond the exploitation of our natural resources, through the period when conservation is essential, and into the stage of the management of resources. Engineering has invaluable contributions to make toward the solution of our social problems caused by population congestions, traffic speed and complexity, and natural disasters. As in so many other fields, the invention of the computer has revolutionized engineering. Systems research, for example, has made possible the revision of factories and transportation, and the beginning of travel in space. A glance at the want ads for engineers in the *New York Times* will show how the demands have changed. Some schools of engineering have been increasing the enrollment of women.

Other of the male-oriented professional schools are shifting their policies toward accepting more women students. The University of Michigan provides good examples. In dentistry, in 1972, there were seven women, a tiny number in the entering class, but a big increase over previous enrollments. In pharmacy, the first-year class had 55 percent women; ten years ago the ratio stood 80 percent men, 20 percent women. In architecture the number of women admitted was nearly doubled over earlier years, although the total was still only 12 percent.

Finally, among the professions, the medical schools are gradually opening their doors a bit wider. In the admissions to medical schools, two trends are quite noticeable. The number of applications from women has doubled during recent years, and the schools have doubled their rate of acceptance of women in about twenty years. In 1971–72, the women in the entering group increased to 13.6 percent. And at Michigan, the entering class of 1972 had 20 percent women.

One of the arguments against educating women in medicine or dentistry has been that they do not remain in practice. In a survey made in 1969, it was found that 84.3 percent of women physicians were active. An additional 1037 women physicians were temporarily out of practice and intended to resume their professional work. If they are added, the percentage becomes 88.6. Women have a higher dropout rate than men, but the charge that women "do not continue as physicians" simply is not true. The majority of women physicians (76.6 percent) are married but marriage does not seem to have a large effect upon continuity of practice.

Interestingly, medicine and dentistry are not regarded as male professions in many countries. Table 7 shows some examples. The contrast between the situation in other countries and in the United States is startling.

Discrimination also exists in politics. For example, in 1969 a newly elected President of the United States had the opportunity to make three hundred top-level appointments in the federal government. He included only thirteen women, three of them White House secretaries. Within the

7. WOMEN AS PERCENT OF TOTAL PROFESSIONAL MEDICAL
PERSONNEL, SELECTED COUNTRIES, 1965

	Physicians	Dentists
Soviet Union	65%	83%
Poland	30	77
Italy	19	—
United Kingdom	16	7
Denmark	16	70
Sweden	15	25
France	13	25
India	12	4
United States	7	2

Source: John B. Parrish, "Women in Medicine: What Can International Comparisons Tell
    Us?" *The Woman Physician* 26–27 (July 1971), 352–61.

next three years he had to fill four vacancies on the United States Supreme Court but failed to nominate any women. No president has ever
nominated a woman for the Court, although there are qualified women
with legal and judicial experience. Also, women outnumber men among
the voters, own a substantial segment of the wealth of the country, and
have superior knowledge about public education, child labor legislation,
slum clearance, and the health and welfare of the people. They should
be more fully represented in elective and appointive political offices.

Women do not get paid salaries equivalent to those of men. For
example, in colleges and universities, in every type of institution, public
and private, women faculty get lower annual salaries than do men in
comparable positions. The National Education Association reported that
for the year 1971–72, the four-year institutions paid women on the
average 19 percent less than men, and two-year colleges paid them 31
percent less. Another example is provided among scientists. In 1970 the
median salary for men was $16,456, for women $13,958, a difference of
15 percent. The rationalization of the margin in favor of the men has
been that the men have more dependents to support. This, however,
dates from the time when a college-educated career woman did not
marry. Today she marries and deposits her check in the joint bank
account. A more likely explanation is that the employers can get away
with it. In the competition for jobs, the woman accepts the lesser pay.
She may have to when she is a captive in an area where her husband is
employed.

In the face of such heavy discrimination what should college women do? Will women students who are now in college encounter as much discrimination when they seek future employment? There is hope. During the last ten years women have become more conscious of the discrimination against them and are fighting more vigorously for change. A number of trends in relieving discriminatory practices are perceptible. For one thing there is coming to be much support for equality of opportunity through recently enacted laws. The state legislatures have been repealing anachronisms in the laws, and enacting laws to prohibit discriminations, such as California's new law on public school employment. The Civil Rights Act of 1964 made relevant declarations, although faculty in educational institutions were excluded. By executive order in 1968 the federal government now forbids contractors with the government from discriminating in employment on the basis of sex. Fifteen or more states have fair employment practices acts which enable persons who feel they have grievances to seek redress. One by one the laws that discriminate against women are being attacked in the courts and are being struck down. The United States Supreme Court in a 1971 ruling declared that pension plans that compel women employees to retire at an earlier age than men are a violation of federal civil rights laws. In 1967, the United Nations made a declaration condemning discrimination against women; unfortunately the United States did not sign it. Congress, however, in 1972 passed a constitutional amendment calling for equal rights and submitted it to the states for approval. As of 1974, more than thirty states had ratified it. For women in general, social change is taking place.

Consorting with the "Enemy"

IFE for a woman is complicated because she is always consorting with a man. Some women even feel that they benefit from the inequality between women and men. The protective arm of the man gives these women a feeling of security. They have no desire to share in or take the responsibility of earning a living. They enjoy having flexibility in the use of leisure. Those women have no desire for change. They represent a long tradition concerning the place of women.

The attitude of college-educated women is usually very different. For example, the trend among them is strongly in favor of marriage plus career. Some women believe that the whole relationship between women and men should be reordered. These changes in attitudes are reflected in the views of women now in college. Of the freshman women surveyed by SCOPE (described in Chapter 4), 69 percent expect to be employed after marriage, and only 3 percent expect to work only before marriage; 28 percent said that they were unsure at this time. Of those who expect to be employed, 11 percent expect to be employed after marriage only until children are born, but 33 percent expect to work both before having children and after they are raised. An additional 18 percent expect to work full-time, and 7 percent part-time for the major part of their lives. When these freshmen were asked whether they wished they "didn't have to work at all," only 9 percent agreed with the statement. Two-thirds of the women said that this was not at all descriptive of them.

Most educated women will continue to be wives and mothers, but they will also want to be doing something else with their lives as well. The educated woman gets a gratification from using her education. Her income makes life easier for the married couple. Both women and men get personal fulfillment from an occupation or profession that engages them continuously after college. Why then should men be so employed, but not women, the women ask.

The dilemma of choosing between home and career, or of preparing for both, should be faced while you are in college. If you decide to devote yourself to establishing and maintaing a good home, you know that you will have the general approval of society and you will find many satisfactions, at least at the present time. But will you have your own approval? Will you find the gratification of exploiting your own potential? And in the end, wouldn't society benefit from your productivity? Wouldn't your husband benefit from your personal growth and development? At age thirty most women will have given birth to their last child, at thirty-five all of the children are likely to be in school. Isn't it possible that twenty-five years from now, the college woman who does not have a career will be looked down upon?

The determining factor in whether a woman is going to follow tradition and custom, or is going to develop her potential, begins to operate early in her life. Parents traditionally conditioned and protected their daughters by different standards than they applied to their sons. Grandparents got into the act and added their influence. The stories the girl read and the games she played were for girls. The girl's days were spent in a woman's world, with her mother's women friends, her mother's women neighbors, and her mother's women relatives. She might hear her elders complain of their role, criticize their husbands, she might hear them attacking the men in their lives; but she rarely heard them plan or work to get out of the role assigned to them. In fact, she was taught her place in that role. She was also taught the taboos relating to it, such as "Don't educate yourself out of the marriage market." She was so brainwashed for the role that she could hardly wait to rush into it. If her repressive conditioning was not so extreme, other influences bombarded her from other sides. On television and in the movies she was shown the stereotyped female ranging from the deified mother to the glamorized plaything, and she was made to like it, to strive to achieve it.

What about the husband? Traditionally he wants a wife to make a home for him. He visualizes the kind of home that mother used to keep.

He, too, has been conditioned for his role as head of the family. Most men consider their wives to be responsible for the daily care and proper upbringing of the children. This is what men are accustomed to. In earlier generations, the moral education of the young was the mother's duty, and this belief hangs on in some families. In addition, some husbands use their homes and the social skills of their wives to support their own ambitions as they rise in responsibility. The ideal wife for such a husband is one who entertains his clients or business associates graciously. The upward mobility of the family may depend upon the manner in which the wife is able to play the role as hostess. This gives her a certain importance and dignity, and for some women this has been and may be enough. She benefits from the rise of the family in social visibility and prestige.

But for other women this kind of life leads to the bridge-playing/martini-consumption syndrome. No wonder that Betty Friedan in her book *The Feminine Mystique* likens the home to a concentration camp. She says that college educates a woman to be free, but then she finds herself subordinated to her husband, his ambitions, his social life; and tied to the home with her apron strings. One woman remarked that it is hard to get freedom because you are always consorting with the enemy.

The question that every girl should ask herself, especially as she prepares to go to college, is how she can live with a man without losing her own identity. Of course, there are some women who don't wish to live with a man. In business or a profession they may want to be partners, perhaps competitors, and perhaps conquerors. But for other women who want a husband, want love and sex and a home, how far can consorting go without bringing defeat?

Some women fear failure in a chosen endeavor because it may subject her to ridicule. On the other hand, success in a role perceived as being masculine can lay her open to rejection by men. Most women fear that. But men also live under the fear of failure, not only in their job, but of greater importance, the failure to provide adequately for their family.

Though some women would not admit it, women do have more choices than men. They may remain at home and in doing so, they meet with social approval. With proper and careful planning, they can find time for activities outside the home—in civic affairs, the church, or in political or cultural affairs. These activities can be commonplace and superficial, indulged in as social pastimes, or they can have career possibilities. We Americans habitually think of vocation as a job that pays a salary, but John Dewey, the philosopher, defined vocation as the activity that is the main interest and effort of an individual. Community service has this potential. Some women view community activities as a relegation of women to nonpaid services. On the other hand, we might have better communities if men joined with women more fully in these activities. As a citizen you have a responsibility to vote, but you may also engage in political and social activism.

In addition, many women today pursue part-time or full-time occupations outside the home that bring into the home not only the financial benefits of their efforts, but the health and harmony that result from the satisfying use of all their capabilities. What are some of these occupations? Which have proven more compatible with a husband, a family?

One factor to consider is the need for mobility. Until women have achieved equal economic responsibility with their husbands for their home and family, most of them will probably continue to let their husband's employment take priority over their own. This means that a woman must be mobile, and able to move to another community when her husband changes the location of his job. When a woman has this problem, she can, of course, solve it by acquiring secretarial, library, nursing, or teaching skills. The newer area of work with computers is open everywhere to a woman who is well trained. These jobs serve a purpose, but ordinarily this type of woman does not enjoy a career in the sense that her husband does.

The woman-man relationship is facilitated when both members of the team are engaged in the same professional area—medicine or law, for example. They can practice separately, or establish an office together. The operation of a joint venture should not be overlooked. In a bookstore, art gallery, or gourmet foods shop or restaurant, or in a vineyard or a strawberry farm, the contributions of the woman and the man are of equal value. Working together to make the venture succeed can be a rewarding life, although admittedly the work can also lead to conflicts if one or the other partner fails to maintain the team spirit.

Many women yearn for the kind of home that men want. A woman may feel that her finest role in life is the creation of a family, and that her greatest responsibility is the care and development of children. There is no social responsibility that is more important. But why does that mean that she must abandon her own destiny? It would help, of course, if society placed a high value upon home management, but society does not. The higher value is placed on professional work and so the laurels go to the husband and his career. This attitude often pushes a woman to choose a career for herself in relation to her interests and abilities, and on its merits, with no consideration of how it will work in marriage.

In college, Margaret studied dramatic art. She was very good at it, good enough to get a part in a New York play that had a successful run of six months. Then she married and had one child (she later had three more). She loved acting, as did two women classmates who later achieved fame on the stage and in television. Naturally she thought about their glamorous life a great deal. But she found that a stage career involved being away from her husband and child night after night. The acting was hard physically, and also produced a degree of nervous tension. Presently she realized that she was living two lives and that strain was developing between them. Reluctantly, she gave up the acting. Now at age forty, with the children well along in school, her need to give them constant attention has diminished. Although she has more freedom of time, and does some acting in local productions, she has continuing concerns about her life with her husband. But she is also restless because she has no consuming activity. She has asked herself, "Should I resume my acting career? Will the night work interfere with the good adjustment Jim and I have achieved? Perhaps I should try to get a job doing some other kind of work that would use my talents."

An alternative for the woman who is not a full devotee of the women's lib movement is to choose a career that will harmonize well with the home responsibilities and to which she can easily return after temporary absences. A career that involves work with children, in libraries or schools, or in health services or nutrition, can be similar in nature to what the woman does in her home, making use of at least some of her special training.

Jill, for example, is married and has a one-year-old son. At college she was trained in special education, which is concerned with teaching children who have disabilities for ordinary learning. Her husband, in a new job, has to be away from home for long hours each weekday. Jill lived in a large Victorian house and decided to start a small nursery school. As a result, she has company for her own child and he requires less of her attention, she earns some money, she is not as lonely as she had been, and she has an incentive to keep abreast of developments in her field. She does not use all of the skills that she learned in college, nevertheless the experience will give her additional background for later reentry into her special field.

Other examples of work that involve children are pediatrician, playground supervisor, children's librarian, day-care program personnel, and photographer who specializes in pictures of children. Alexandra was trained as a pediatrician. She is in a profession in which she can establish her own office hours and thus space her absences from homes so that she can be with her family when they need her most. In other words, she works by an appointment schedule and thus controls her own time. Since her husband also works, the money she earns—and the income of a pediatrician is not small—adds to the sum that is available for extra things, including babysitters, near-complete laundry service, and dinners out with her husband. She also knows the latest about bringing up her own children.

The woman who is both home manager and full-time professional career woman may find that she is carrying a considerable overload of work, demanding in time and sometimes requiring creative thinking of a type that cannot be done after a fatiguing day either at the office, or in the home. The social entertaining to promote the career of either her husband or herself continues to fall most heavily upon her. When both the wife and the husband return from work much fatigued, the home may deteriorate in quality. Perhaps this accounts for the high divorce rate among professional women.

What every working wife needs is a supportive husband. One type of supportive husband has been well described by Lettie Cottin Pogrebin in her book *How To Make It in a Man's World*. Ms. Pogrebin is a career woman who reached the executive level with a publishing firm at an unusually early age. Her job was demanding in time and energy, yet she found time to have a family. She defined a good husband for the working woman as ". . . the kind of guy who will pick you up at the office because your briefcase is too heavily loaded and your shoes pinch, foot the bill for the most competent babysitter that money can buy, get up at 4 a.m. to give a relief bottle even though you both have to work the next day, take the kids out for a whole Sunday so that you can catch up on your work, treat you to a restaurant dinner because you're too pooped to cook."

When a woman chooses a career on its merits, a consideration is whether the job pattern can be modified to accommodate the needs of a married woman in a life-style comfortable for her. Changing a job pattern involves, at the minimum, leaves of absence for childbirth and for family emergencies, plus provision for child care in centers conveniently located for the parents' use and sufficiently well run to be satisfactory as a place in which to leave preschool children. The child care center movement is gaining more public acceptance and sponsorship by governmental agencies.

Further reforms of two types may become possible. One is that work schedules will be revised so as to enable the family-minded woman to coordinate her activities at home with those on the job. The daily schedule might be revised to permit her to be on the job or at her office during the hours that her children do not require her attention or are in school. For example, the head of the national business conditions section of the Federal Reserve Bank in Boston, a woman with a young child, has been permitted to rearrange her schedule so that she now works twenty hours per week instead of the former thirty-six, and for five-ninths of her former salary. In view of trends toward shorter work days and weeks, this reform of work schedules would seem practical. The other reform— a sharing of the home duties by husband and wife—is becoming more customary. This sharing of work in the home actually began when women began to enter the outside work force in substantial numbers. The trend may now be considerably accelerated because of the belief of youth that they should not be bound by traditional patterns of wife-husband relationships. The attitudes of the young men are crucial, because a revision of home life depends upon the acceptance by the man that home and children are their joint responsibility. When this relationship prevails, the husband and wife may engage equally in careers.

But will your husband retrogress into the pattern of home life he learned as a child? This is one of the risks. College graduates commonly do regress to their old habit patterns; they revert to watching the popular television programs and reading the news magazines, leading a competitive social life, and accepting without analysis the customs and mores of their environment. The answer in your case will depend in part upon the degree of resolution you and your husband achieve and your success in establishing a new pattern of living that presently becomes an habitual one.

It will help greatly in the resolution of some of these dilemmas if the care of the home becomes professionalized. Fewer women are becoming maids. Maid service involves drudgery, is ill-paid and demeaning. As the young women from the lower socioeconomic segments of the population become better educated and absorbed into employment as secretaries, air stewardesses, sales clerks, data processors, bank tellers, and other positions of higher prestige and salaries than maid service, few of them will desire to become maids. On the other hand, assuming better incomes, some women may become caterers and home service personnel. On a differently organized basis that recognizes the dignity and worth of the services, some of the meal services and much of the laundry, cleaning, and maintenance work might be done by this new class of professionals. If the educated woman is to avoid becoming more bound to the home than ever because of the absence of maids, she must participate in bringing about a change in the patterns of rendering household services.

The woman who takes time out to raise a family needs to anticipate that she may have some problems with retraining and reentry to a job. There is no good reason why a woman should permanently give up her plans for a career. The expenditure for education by her and by the college has been large. Hence, the social waste involved in her not working is substantial. As noted in Chapter 8, in the case of physicians a high percentage of women physicians remain active. It seems probable that in the future educated women will continue, with few exceptions, in their jobs or professional careers or return to them after temporary absences.

If a woman has been out a few years, she has the problem of finding a new job. This is not easy to do. It would have been wiser to retain a connection, if only part time. Often a serious problem arises from a failure to keep alert to developments in the field of work or to keep one's skills in condition. Some of the knowledge acquired years ago will have become superseded by more recent findings and theories. But even where the knowledge has remained valid her memory of it may need to be refreshed, and her skills may have deteriorated through lack of use. Hence, a person who does not refresh herself after an absence may be unemployable.

Fortunately, the colleges and professional schools recognize the need for retraining programs. A number of universities have established centers of continuing education for women. The enrollee is assisted by counselors to find the best courses to expedite employment and to gain acceptance in them as a student. These centers also help women regain confidence in their abilities and themselves. Information about these programs can easily be obtained by writing to a university.

The possibility that you may have to take a leave from your work has an implication about the manner in which you should study in college. It is important to learn how to learn, and cultivate the habit of continuous learning. If you know how to learn, you will have the ability to refresh yourself, or prepare for a new occupation.

A woman student has much more difficult decisions to make about preparation for a career and about the kind of life she wants to live than has a man. As shown above, there is a host of considerations to take into account. At stake is not only the future career itself but also the mode of family living and management, and personal adjustments in a society that is divided as to the proper place of woman.

10

Who Am I?

*S*ARAH arrived at college on Tuesday. Her parents had driven her to the campus, five hundred miles from home. She came bringing her clothes, her stereo set, and her bicycle. Sarah was excited about going away to this particular college. A favorite friend of hers in the civic theatre group was an alumna and Sarah, too, was planning on majoring in dramatic arts. Her parents stayed at a motel nearby until she was settled.

On Friday morning, Sarah was back in the family car with her suitcases, her stereo set, and her bicycle, on her way home. What had happened?

Sarah said she didn't know. For the two or three days that she had been on campus she had talked to some of the other young women who were also freshmen. They were eager to start classes and excited about what the year would bring. But Sarah, after arriving, had doubts about being at college. Why was she here? Did she belong here? She decided she had to leave. Her mother said, "Why not stay for a semester? Give yourself a chance to see what it's like." Her father was at a loss. He tried to remember his first few days at the university. There had been confusion and apprehension, but there was no question about his remaining. Maybe girls were different.

Sarah was trying to explain. "Why should we spend all this money on tuition when I don't know whether I should be here? Am *I* really great actress material? Mom, Dad, please—I have to go home and get my head straightened out before I can do anything. If I stay here, I know I just couldn't study."

At eighteen, Sarah at college would be on her own for the first time. Last year she was so confident—now she wondered about leaving everyone she knew. Did she really want to be an actress? Could she make it? What kinds of decisions would she have to make about herself now? And what about Chester? Would he miss her or would he find someone else at Yale? These were some of the personal problems that suddenly confronted Sarah as she arrived at college. They have to do with her concern about what she wants to do and who she wants to be. So Sarah left to work out her identity crisis at home.

Have you ever asked yourself, "How did I become ME, this person?" "How do I look to others?" "What is this core within me that makes me what I am and different from everyone else?"

You, like everyone else, have an inner identity in addition to the outer one described on your driver's license—the intangible identity that makes you, you. Identity is difficult to describe, since it is at the same time an abstraction, a feeling, and an existence. It is the decisive determinant of the inner quality of life. It is knowing who you are as a unique individual and as a member of a larger group. It is both psychological and social. Identity is the nucleus of the personality.

Identities are formed like mosaics, with many events and influences contributing to the formation. Some characteristics of identity come from subidentities. A woman, for instance, is not only herself as she sees herself—a person different from all other persons—but, as a member of the female sex, she has a sexual identity different from her brother. As a college student, she has a family identity distinct from the young woman sitting beside her in class. Although she may have a different self-image in a calculus class where she has just failed a quiz than she has tutoring her younger brother in arithmetic, there is an inner core in her—an abiding sense of self—a personal identity. Contributing strongly to her identity are those beliefs and values formed early in life.

Erik Erikson is perhaps the foremost psychologist writing on this subject. He describes identity as how the person sees and thinks of herself in relation to her world and how she judges herself in the light of how she thinks others judge her. Identity is not static but rather a continuing process. It forms as the person advances through predetermined stages depending upon her readiness and ability to move into new situations and to deal with other individuals. In moving forward, the person changes and develops by her responses to experiences and by combining these new experiences with what has gone before. In the beginning, of course, the identity develops with the mother or the mother substitute. Many other factors also influence and mold identity: events over which the person has no control, learned responses, identification with father and other important people as well as mother, and one's own inner reactions to external events. Equally important in forming the identity of a woman are the subtle emotional overtones of anxiety, approval, anger, affection, pride, or sexual tension that accompany the words and actions of those people who are significant to her during her childhood and adolescence. Despite this continual modification, identity is based on her knowing and perceiving herself as the same today, tomorrow, and continuing on into time until death. Her family and friends, too, recognize this sameness and continuity in her as they do in themselves.

During infancy and childhood, identity formation occurs unconsciously. At adolescence, when the individual has the necessary physiological and psychological growth, and is on the verge of adulthood, the identity crisis occurs. The word *crisis* is used not to signify a time of turmoil but a necessary turning point in the development of the individual. The crisis may come on gradually and be resolved tranquilly; or it may bring with it a period of anxiety and conflict. It is an interim period during which the adolescent will make decisions important to the emerging adult. That is why adolescents like to join cliques and groups, because they offer opportunities to try out various roles, and in addition, offer the rewards of "belonging." In order to belong, to secure approval and to be accepted, the members may be subtly coerced into meeting the group's standards. This is the time when to be different is to be suspect, when there is security and acceptance in being the same as one's peers. During the identity crisis, adolescents may be emotional and inconsistent. They may have mood changes, swinging from feelings of maturity and independence to feelings of insecurity and uncertainty. But sometimes this conflict helps them to grow stronger as they test themselves between these two positions.

This period of the identity crisis between adolescence and adulthood Erikson terms a *moratorium*. Some persons, unable to attain a sense of confidence in an adult identity, choose to prolong the period of moratorium and continue in the guise of a pseudo-identity. Some remain at this stage for the rest of their lives; others work through this period and emerge at a later time with a sense of oneness with their inner selves. A negative identity is a form of regression to an earlier stage in a person's development. Erikson defines a negative identity as "identity perversely based on all those identifications and roles which at critical stages of development, had been presented as most undesirable or dangerous and yet also as most real." This was aptly illustrated in bygone days by the preacher who made sin and fornication so real that his son became a playboy. The young person who chooses a negative identity may become alienated from society and drop out. She may turn to drugs, sex, or a different life-style. Her efforts are directed toward defining herself as *someone*. Some people adopt a negative identity because they cannot accept the role expected of them by society and/or their family. Some may feel that what they are not supposed to be is so clearly defined that it is easier to be that than to struggle with the feeling of unreality in roles which they think they cannot attain or which fail to meet their inner needs.

In theory, when the adolescent girl surmounts the period of identity crisis, and bridges the gap between adolescence and adulthood, she finds her own niche and achieves a comfortable internal feeling of sameness and continuity. She has a sense of well-being and a desire to enter into the adult world and take on its challenges and responsibilities. In practice, identity formation does not always work out so smoothly.

Psychologists differ about women's identity crises. Some believe that women, in general, have a serene adolescence and emerge into adulthood easily; others hold that women do not achieve their identity readily. Rather, women find their sense of confidence and identity later than men and only after they have fulfilled their traditional roles of wife and mother. Certainly much of these latter feelings are reflections of the expectations of society—expectations which are now undergoing examination and evaluation.

Ideally, a child's identity would be formed in a loving and positive manner. Ideally, her internal reactions to events would be such as to channel her toward assuming adulthood smoothly. Yet there is still much to learn about the determinants of psychological and personality development. Why is it, for instance, that similar events can produce different experiences in children born and raised in the same family? What is it that makes one child become a surgeon and the other an alcoholic?

Although the identity crisis is a normative occurrence, its resolution does not always progress in a consistently positive manner. Identity confusion is experienced and may be evidenced by difficulties in forming intimate relationships, in working toward a career, in handling time, and in the ability to concentrate; or conversely, in investing all of one's energies into a single activity such as painting or reading. College students particularly feel pressed toward making many decisions all at once—relationships with the opposite sex, handling their own sexuality, preparing for careers, intimacy with roommates and peers, and living up to expectations of families and friends.

Sarah, under the pressures of the identity crisis, was in a state of confusion. Her early years were normal and happy ones. As the only girl in a family of two brothers and six cousins, her feminine characteristics were admired at family gatherings. One of these was her enjoyment in dressing up in costumes and acting out stories to her audience. The family's response to her in these roles encouraged her to continue. In school, she was assigned parts because of her assurance in the actress role. Without any thoughtful evaluation of what talents she had or needed, Sarah and her family fell into the assumption that she would study dramatics. At college, when faced with the finality of this decision and the competition of dedicated drama majors, Sarah belatedly realized that she had never honestly evaluated her abilities or thought out who she wanted to be or what she wanted to do with her life.

Sarah's early identity developed in a loving environment. Her relationships with her parents and brothers were easy. The purpose of her life, though, was never something she gave conscious thought to. Perhaps her family's acceptance and expectations of her as the pretty, pleasant, passive child were contributing factors. Sarah's choice of a vocation was not the result of an intrinsic motivation, but rather, something laid upon her. Nevertheless, a complex of reasons made Sarah leave the college abruptly. She was overcome with apprehensions—leaving her parents for the first time, living with many young women all seemingly so assured about their careers, and of course, leaving her boyfriend, after they had been inseparable for two years.

After Sarah had returned home she obtained a job as a clerk with the gas and electric company in an office handling customer complaints. Sarah did a good job and she related well to people. In the spring she was asked to take a better, supervisory position. By that time, however, she had decided that she was ready for college and had been accepted to a liberal arts college for the fall semester. She planned to major in

English as she liked to write and also, she was considering teaching English and speech in high school. Sarah no longer felt she wanted only to be with Chester, and she had been dating some of the young men where she worked. She said that she didn't want to get deeply involved with one man until she had practiced being herself for a while. After taking a half a year to think about herself, Sarah believed she had attained a feeling of identity and inner purpose.

Jennifer, also a college student, describes her identity confusion (more severe than Sarah's) during the year following her freshman year in college. Below is an excerpt from an interview:

JENNIFER: At the end of the semester, I didn't want to go home. There were a lot of things that went into that: guilt, disappointment at my parents' end and picking it up and making it mine. Those feelings of guilt.

INTERVIEWER: Because of poor grades?

J: Uh, huh, because I felt that I hadn't done what I was supposed to have done. I felt that I hadn't measured up. They had set a certain standard for me and I had picked up on it and made it my standard. Whether I wanted to or not, I don't know. But I hadn't thought about whether I wanted to or not. I just picked it up and made it my standard. And I hadn't lived up to it and I was guilty. I was feeling guilty. My self-esteem was very low. I was seriously questioning myself as a person. It was a hard time for me. My mother has said to me since then, about a year later, "When you came home," she said, "it was incredible, my heart went out to you. Because you seemed to be in so much turmoil," which I was. Questioning everything, looking at everything, taking it apart and looking at it, then putting it back together again was a very slow process. . . . But I did come home. . . . And being at home for the next year or until the folks moved to the east coast, which was in March, was a depressing time. I didn't get into much. I went to a local college and took two courses and worked thirty hours a week in a department store. Straight through until we moved.

And there weren't too many people that I knew that were still home. Most were at school. It was a depressing time for me.

I: Tell me about it. How did you work your way out of it? What happened?

J: I didn't. Until we moved. I just hung in there and was satisfied with . . . just kind of hibernating in my depression . . . not thinking too much about it one way or the other. It's depressing for me to think about it now, it wasn't that long ago. I kept a diary of sorts and in rereading it, I find it was very depressing, very disparaging.

I: Disparaging of yourself? Your parents?

J: Yes. Of everything. It's a down for me to read it now. It was hurt and it was pain, it was sadness. Very little joy. My writing . . . was one of my ways of getting it out of myself. I spent a lot of that time also crying on my guy's shoulder about how mean and what monsters my parents were. That was my . . . get-back-at-the-folks-for-everything-they've-ever-done-to-you year. I just chose to blame my parents for the way I Was and Where I Was At. And I was content to do that, until we moved.

I was in New Jersey for two weeks and decided I was going to split. I just decided that . . . I was scared and I wanted to run away. And I ran back to Illinois.

In doing that, from that point, from the day that I left New Jersey and went back to Illinois—things changed.

And it started a snowballing effect on everything, all the things that I had taken apart and were lying in bits and pieces around me, pieces of myself that I had succeeded in taking apart and looking at but hadn't quite known how to put together, and in what place to put them in when I got them together. And I started to find myself, as a person.

Whether it was necessary for me to completely and physically remove myself from my parents, you know, half way across the states—it seemed to be necessary at that time. As well as running away from something, I was running to something. And what I think now, was that was myself and my idea that I might find myself, which I did start to do. And I was living with a guy. I decided that I wasn't ready to live with a guy, wasn't ready to live in that kind of a relationship yet. There were too many things that I had to do by myself, with myself, before I could be in a place where I could take on somebody else's self.

And I lived there for two months, at which time I decided that I couldn't successfully within a reasonable amount of time go back to school. I didn't have the money. I would have had to work a year, go to school a year . . . done something like that. Gone to school part-time, worked part-time. I wanted to do it now. My choice was to go home. And do it. I could go to school free that way.

So that was my . . . the turning point of my life. That's the place in my life . . . in which I found I was the only person responsible for me. There was nobody else in the world responsible for me except me. And all in that same idea which was just a beautiful revelation, I stopped blaming my parents, there was no such thing as blame. I completely lost the concept of blame and what it meant. My parents became people to me. I took on myself and all the responsibilities that I have to myself as a person, and realized that they were all mine and belong to nobody else except me. And I could make of them whatever I chose. Whatever I chose to do with them, was my choosing and my doing. Right now, I'm my life.

Early in her freshman year, Jennifer tried to find out more about herself through drugs, as many of her peers were doing. A description of that phase of her college life will be resumed later.

Everyone does not automatically achieve a sense of well-being upon arriving at adulthood irrespective of whether her identity crisis passes smoothly or tumultuously. Some women feel a deep and pervasive sense of insecurity. This need not be a lifelong detriment. Carl Rogers, noted psychotherapist, among others, believes that people can change themselves throughout life if they desire to do so. Erikson, too, believes that one's identity can be developed and improved. A damaged psyche can be healed or a weak identity strengthened through psychotherapy, counseling, reading, and self-analysis. Determination can accomplish great things. One autobiography, written as part of the admission process to college, presented a positive picture of a young woman sure of fulfilling her ambitions. Her father was schizophrenic and went into protracted rages. Her mother had to work to contribute to their support. But all that made the young woman more determined. Studying at home would be difficult and so she wanted to live on campus. "I am responsible for myself," she wrote, "I can be the victim or the heroine of my life. I am striving to be the heroine."

College need not be deferred because you are unsure of what you want to achieve in life. One of the major purposes of college is to help you to prepare for a satisfying life. College offers a fresh environment and will provide you with many stimulations to excite your interest. Colleges have many resources—teachers, counselors, libraries—that can help you to find answers to your questions. It has courses to assist you to learn more about yourself as a human being. It can help you to identify a career and prepare for it. At college, you will meet many new and congenial friends. You may have left someone at home whom you think of as a lifelong companion, but you may find in college an enlarged world and a greater selection of harmonious companions, both female and male.

Many students say that they learned more about themselves in their rap sessions in college residences than they had in their four years of high school. In college, they had a large group of peers who knew, understood, and could relate to their problems and who had the time, place, and inclination to discuss and dissect them.

As stated earlier, the identity crisis need not be a time of tumult. Psychologists who have studied college students find that the majority work through this period uneventfully.

‖|‖

Sex on Campus—An
All-American Thing?

‖WENTY years ago an unmarried college woman who was not a virgin did not talk about it. Fifty years ago it was a shameful predicament. But today sexual experience is openly discussed by college women. Now it is the virgin who may be placed on the defensive by her peers. Despite this open and free climate, many young women lack accurate information about sex and worry about their life-style.

Do you feel assured about your own sexual behavior? Have you found answers to your questions about sex? At home you were pretty much in command of yourself. As a senior in high school you were known, accepted, and secure in familiar surroundings. In college, especially if you are far from home, you may be homesick and lonely during the first few weeks. You will be meeting large numbers of new people of your age, and you may be subjected to greater academic competition than you had in high school. In this new environment you may seek a boyfriend with whom kissing and holding is natural; you will feel less homesick and more secure. Moreover, you are at the age when the sexual drive is strong and presses for fulfillment. It is also the period when you are striving to achieve identity, and when acceptance by your peer group is keenly sought. It is a time, then, when you may be pressed to have sex, perhaps unexpectedly. Can you be better prepared to make the right decision, one that is right for you?

The times when a college woman is most vulnerable to having a transitory sexual relationship are when she first goes away to college and when she is especially open to dependent attachments, and following the break-up of a relationship during which she had sex because she believed it to be a lasting affair.

Do all college women have sex? If not, what are the sexual mores on campus? Are there any facts available?

The first carefully documented study of the college population was made in 1948 by Alfred Kinsey, a biologist, head of the Institute for Sex Research at Indiana University. He found that 27 percent of college women and 67 percent of college men were sexually experienced, and reported his findings in *Sexual Behavior in the Human Male* (1948) and *Sexual Behavior in the Human Female* (1953). Ten years later, in 1963, there was little change in the sexual behavior of women college students at Stanford and at Berkeley, according to Joseph Katz and Associates as reported in *No Time for Youth,* a book based on a study of the development of college students over a four-year period. They found that 25 percent of the women had had sex by the middle of the junior year. These women were freshmen in 1961. There is, however, some evidence that women become more active as they progress through college. Harrup and Ruth Freeman, authors of "Senior College Women: Their Sexual Standards and Activity: Parts I and II," in *Journal of the National Association of Women Deans and Counselors* 29 (Spring and Winter 1966) reported that 55 percent of the senior college women they interviewed from 1962 to 1965 said they were sexually experienced. These earlier studies, made before the pill came into widespread use, were in agreement that at least one-fourth of the college women were sexually experienced.

To obtain current information for his book, *The Sexual Wilderness,* Vance Packard in 1966 sent questionnaires to 2100 junior and senior college students in twenty-one colleges and universities throughout the United States. Of the 67 percent responding, 43 percent of the women and 58 percent of the men reported having experienced coitus. As expected, there continued to be an excess of male sexual activity. He discovered that there were also wide differences in behavior by geographical region.

Coital Rates of College Juniors and Seniors

Females

East	57%
West	48%
South	32%
Midwest	25%

Males

South	69%
East	64%
West	62%
Midwest	46%

It is apparent that the south had a more pronounced double standard than other sections of the country. The southern males ranked in the top half of the twenty-one schools as being sexually experienced, and the southern females in the bottom half.

Packard reported other differences: the students in colleges in the rural areas were generally more conservative than those in metropolitan schools, private college students held more permissive attitudes than those in public colleges, but public school males were the more experienced. Students from church-related colleges generally reported a lower percentage of sexual experience than students from nonsectarian colleges. Colleges with liberal rules had a higher proportion of sexually experienced students than schools with conservative rules, but other factors also contribute to this difference. College personnel are aware that liberal students apply to schools with liberal orientations; hence initial selection for college admission is done by students themselves. Schools which permitted the entertainment of guests of the opposite sex in their rooms reported a higher incidence of coital experience than schools that did not. Only four schools in the study permitted visiting; they were all in the northeast.

The acceptance of a double standard by some college students was illustrated by the responses to a question asking whether a sexually experienced man should expect to marry a virgin. Thirty-six percent of the women and 21 percent of the men answered affirmatively. The majority of women and men repudiated the double standard intellectually, but they did not accept the concept of sexual equality emotionally. Thirty-nine percent of the women but 70 percent of the men said they would be seriously or somewhat troubled if their mate were not a virgin.

Since 58 percent of the men reporting said they were sexually experienced, the implication is that some of them nevertheless preferred to marry a virgin.

The students in Packard's study, both female and male, felt strongly that age and emotional maturity had to be taken into consideration in evaluating the appropriateness of sexual acts. This was substantiated by the college women we interviewed who reported that having a relationship with a man which includes sex involves them emotionally and that breaking up has all the trauma of a divorce.

In 1967 Ira L. Reiss, sociologist at Iowa State University and scholar of human sexual behavior, in his book, *The Social Context of Pre-Marital Sexual Permissiveness,* states that, based on his findings, there had been little change in the rates of sexual activity among unmarried youth in the last fifty years. It was their *attitudes,* not their *actions,* that had changed. Dr. Paul Gebhard, successor to Dr. Kinsey as head of the Indiana Institute for Sex Research, affirmed in 1969 that there was no revolution in sex activity on United States campuses but, rather, a continuation of a trend whereby each succeeding generation has more premarital intercourse than the previous one.

The authors of this book, however, on the basis of their interviewing, have received the impression that there has been a sexual revolution on the campuses, both in attitude and behavior of college students. We believe that sexual experience and not virginity is the reality with the majority of college women. Also, when an unmarried woman and man live together, they openly admit it.

The 1972 report of the Presidential Commission on Population Growth and the American Future bears out the contention that there has been recently a strong trend toward increased sexual activity by very young women. They found that "nearly half of all unmarried women have had sexual intercourse by the time they are 19 years old and most of them have run high risks of becoming pregnant."

While these studies indicate increased premarital sexual activity on the part of young women, college women generally are not promiscuous. Our interviewing revealed that the attitudes of individual women were restrained even when they had had sexual experience. They said they have sex when they have a meaningful relationship and when an expression of love seemed to be the natural thing. The same can be said for high school students, at least on the west coast. Many date one person exclusively which is referred to as "going together" rather than "going steady," and which implies engagement and marriage. Some couples who go together have sex, but high school students do not condone promiscuity—in girls. Girls in one high school who sleep around are called "sluts" and have "reputations." The double standard still exists. Notwithstanding the acceptance of sexual behavior by many high school students, disclosures during sex raps give evidence that many young women submit to having sex before they are ready or entirely willing. Counselors of teen-age groups report that many young women who don't want to have sex are able to adhere to their decisions by bringing their feelings into the open in these discussions. In effect, they receive permission from the group to determine their own behavior. Also, we found that virginity is still prized by some women who are genuinely desirous of remaining chaste before marriage. These young women have varying reasons for remaining celibate. Some devote themselves to study, others believe that a wife's virginity contributes to a good and lasting marriage. Some believe they have something unique and use it as a weapon: "I have saved myself for you and therefore you must regard me as something special and precious."

Nevertheless, there are some young women who prefer not to get involved with men early in their academic careers. The most serious intellectual students often tend to identify more with the faculty and their academic interests than with their peers. In the Stanford-Berkeley study rather a large number of students, about one-quarter of them, reported little or no dating during their high school and college years. At Stanford University where, at that time the ratio of students was two and a half men to every woman, over 20 percent of the women students reported having no dates in an average week during the four years of college.

Even those young women in the 1970s who do date seem to be placing less emphasis on dating for marriage than their older sisters did. Early marriage is no longer the vogue. Teenage marriages, for example, have dropped from the high of 25 percent reached in 1955 to 17 percent in 1970 according to the United States Bureau of the Census. Previously, highly educated women were less apt to marry; now most women do marry, but at a later age. Career women are marrying after they complete their studies and are increasingly marrying men in their own field. Most of the women we interviewed said they would want to live with a man before they could commit themselves with a legal ceremony.

Do men have the same desires regarding fidelity in a relationship that women have? Reports of research on sexual practices prior to the 1970s revealed that men had sexual intercourse with women for whom they didn't have any real concern. Women, on the other hand, confined their sexual relations to men they were in love with. It is evident from studies that men now have intercourse with the women they date on campus, rather than with prostitutes. According to Packard, college males' experience with prostitutes had dropped to 4 percent in 1966 from the 22 percent reported by Kinsey in 1948. Even at the high-school level there is some indication of a trend in boys on the west coast to prefer to "go together" with one girl rather than to sleep around.

In the past, males have been oriented toward premarital sex *per se,* and sexual experiences for them have been accepted and expected; but for females oriented toward love, sexual experiences were condemned. According to one researcher, males have a number of slang terms to describe the female and male genitalia, whereas women's vocabulary regarding sex is romantic in nature. Men think of women in terms of stereotypes, women think of men as individuals. One of the statements made in the Stanford-Berkeley study was that women achieved a more mature orientation to sex because they are apparently more aware of the psychological complexities involved. Men are more prone to action, and a third of the senior-year men in the study seemed to think of women primarily as sex objects. This would appear to substantiate the general belief that college men look forward to each class of incoming freshmen as virgin territory. Often, before the gullible freshman knows what is happening, she is rushed off her feet and into a prone position. Too late, she may find that the experience was not what she wanted or that her erstwhile friend is now playing a duet with the music major down the hall.

Regardless of the moral standards of the time, and despite even harsh and punitive action, society has never been able to eliminate premarital sex completely. Nevertheless, right and wrong behavior between women and men has been specifically prescribed since the earliest time of civilization. In the United States, sex before marriage has not been considered an acceptable practice for women; men, on the other hand, were expected to be sexually experienced by the time they married. Similarly, a man might have an extramarital fling now and then without losing his reputation if he were circumspect about it, but women who indulged in such behavior were considered wanton and immoral and often ostracized by society. These views were upheld by both sexes.

After the first World War and during the Second, sexual mores became considerably less rigid, for whenever women enter the outside world to work they free themselves of some of the shackles of custom and convention. By the 1960s, the results of permissive child-rearing practices, peer-group influences, the large population in the college-age group, introduction of new birth control methods—principally the pill— and the increasing mobility of youth had all played a part in bringing about changes toward less restrictive codes of sexual morality. These changes did not come about without strife. Parents struggled, and many are struggling still, to maintain their beliefs against the forces of change while their children scrutinize and, in many cases, experiment with new life styles often totally different from their parents'.

Along with these changes came a new social ethic among college students. Dana Farnsworth, then head of Harvard University's student health services, said in 1970 that the new sexual code was well known to college physicians and psychiatrists since they had confidential information from students that gave them a more accurate picture of the college scene than others might obtain. According to him the basic tenets of the new morality were that rightness or wrongness of action should be based upon the circumstances of the case rather than on absolute standards laid down by another generation; and that actions should be nonexploitative and guided by integrity. Within this framework sexual intercourse between persons having a deep commitment was acceptable and considered right by the students.

Some sociologists believe that we are moving toward the Scandinavian pattern of sexual mores where sex with affection is taken for granted and remaining virginal for one's marriage partner unimportant. (A survey of Swedish brides in 1950 indicated that 80 percent were nonvirgins.) The Swedes link sexual freedom to sexual equality; hence in the United States, with the women's liberation movement, sexual mores may be moving in the same direction. There is little likelihood of a reversal to the more restrictive attitude.

A report of a study released in September 1972, however, indicated that both Swedish women and American college women still hold a double-standard attitude toward sex. "In Seattle or in Stockholm, women rarely admit taking the initiative for instigating intercourse; they seldom admit to choosing casual partners, and they are more likely than men to claim marriage or engagement with their partners," according to Hall and Wagner, psychologists at the University of Washington. Being the instigator of the initial contact is evidently a form of behavior young women have not fully accepted. In a study at Miami University in Ohio, college women were asked if they approved of women asking men to whom they are attracted for dates. More than half of the respondents (56 percent) expressed disapproval. Nevertheless, we are living in a time of rapid change and such attitudes may be dissipated in a few years.

Even though society at large no longer holds rigid sexual standards, young women who have had several sexual partners often experience feelings of guilt and confusion. They neither embrace their parents' moral values nor completely disregard them. A university psychiatrist reporting on mental health stated that promiscuity can produce emotional problems and that experiences associated with being promiscuous are stressful and interfere with the development of healthy personality traits. Also, the sexually promiscuous woman comes to see herself more as an object and less as an equal partner. Both Packard and Farnsworth drew similar conclusions.

College women at Stanford and Berkeley, more often than men, worried about what their sexual behavior should be. The students who reported having the greatest struggle over sexual values were the women with the highest dating experience (50 percent of them). Only 11 percent of the men in the highest dating group reported having any pangs of conscience. The Hall and Wagner study cited earlier stated that in both Sweden and the United States the men reported more positive sexual events, more satisfaction, and less remorse than the women.

Women and men base their morality upon several factors: the values of their friends, the values of their parents, and the kind of social group in which they were raised. When a woman goes away to college she removes herself from the social group in which she was brought up, and although her parents' values remain with her they are weakened by the pressures of the new environment. In their study of women college seniors, the Freemans (cited above) reported that the college roommate and the specific male were the factors with the most influence in determining the sexual behavior of college women. In Packard's study the returns from one of the schools, an eastern college, disclosed that 75 percent of the junior and senior women had had sexual encounters. Even by eastern standards this proportion seemed high at that time, and was higher than the other schools in the east which averaged 41 percent. Packard made a personal visit to the school in an effort to discover the reason for the higher figure. The explanation was that to be "in," one had to be sexually experienced. The women discovered this expectation shortly after their arrival and usually managed to have a sexual encounter by the end of their freshman year. This illustration gives evidence of the strong influence of the peer group but not of a good reason for having sex.

Today's college women are more accepting and less critical of diversity in sexual behavior than previous generations of college women have been. Additionally, the new contraceptives have freed women from unwanted pregnancies and have removed a major reason for withholding sexual intercourse until marriage. In some ways these changes have increased the difficulty for women, because they no longer have absolute standards by which to measure and judge their behavior. Some men, and women, too, have construed the sexual revolution as meaning sex on demand, regardless of the degree of closeness or affection. This may account for the unease which the women are experiencing. Instead of feeling liberated, some women feel more enslaved than ever. As stated previously, many young women feel they are being pushed into sex before they want to by their boyfriends and by the whole sexual climate. The women interviewed for this book who were serene about themselves were those who had given thought to their actions. They had sex because they felt it was right at the time. Some had had relations with more than one man, but by and large, they viewed sex as more than a physical need; trust, tenderness, and affection were some of the other necessary ingredients. Arguments in favor of recreational sex are based on the thesis that the genus, man, is an animal and that sex is a natural act. But man is able to stand apart from himself and contemplate his actions. Hence, in order to have true freedom, a woman must feel right about herself when she considers her actions. Whether she remains a virgin, or decides to have a relationship because of a deep attachment, or considers sex a natural act, her primary concern should be how she accepts herself in the context of her actions.

12
Tracey's Story

N interviewing young women about their college experiences, we naturally found some who more than others were interested in sharing. We found some who were more able to open themselves to the kind of searching introspection that was required. And, of course, some more than others were able to talk about themselves articulately, and with insight about their experiences. Tracey's story is given in detail because she was available for several interviews over a period of time, and because she was one of those who was more aware and who could, as well, most successfully be articulate about her conduct and her reactions, and finally, she had reached some conclusions which became part of her philosophy of life.

Tracey is twenty-three. Her father is a physician; her mother is a college graduate; both are practicing Catholics. Tracey is the second of five children; there is an older brother in law school, a sister just starting college, and two younger brothers in high school. The family home is located in a rural-suburban community.

Up to the time that she was graduated from high school, Tracey did not have many social contacts with children other than her sister and brothers. Although she attended a local school, her family went to their lodge in the mountains during weekends and vacations. The lodge, located on a lake, was an ideal retreat for a large family who enjoyed summer and winter sports, reading, and handicrafts. Tracey described her childhood as protected, pleasant, and comfortable. When she was ten her father accepted a post as a consultant in public health in a foreign country. The family remained there for four years. Tracey attended the local school but it was not rigorous. Returning home she was over-whelmed by the rushing, fast-paced American civilization. The school she entered evaluated her ability and her preparation and placed her in classes that were not preparatory for college. She felt pretty inferior, although she was reading Thomas Merton at the time. Notwithstanding this put-down, Tracey graduated in three and a half years with a B+ average.

After graduation from high school, Tracey applied to and was ac-cepted at an excellent liberal arts college in the east, College A. The school was her own choice. She wanted to go away to college, to experi-ence deep friendships with peers outside her family, and to find out about herself. At college, Tracey continued her earlier interest in philosophy although she was in a science curriculum. She also became interested in Freud, the founder of psychoanalysis. Despite her efforts to understand herself and mix with her peers, she found it hard to overcome the feeling of strangeness she had in this permissive college atmosphere. Contempla-tive and shy, Tracey seemed to be looking on from the sidelines. But there was also the other side—experiencing freedom from her family. According to Tracey, her life was either so highly structured by herself or so completely formless that her functioning was minimal. She knew she couldn't get into the "man thing" before finding out about herself, but her insecurity found comfort in a classmate, Doug. They spent most of their time with each other and eventually moved into having a sexual relationship. By the end of the first year, they were sharing an apartment.

During the winter recess in her freshman year, Tracey visited Doug's home. His mother appraised the situation and advised Doug to see that Tracey was taking proper precautions against pregnancy. Up until this time they had been using haphazard methods, so when they returned to college, Tracey phoned her parents to ask them to send a note to the college's medical service giving their permission for her to have birth control pills. Their immediate reaction was negative and emotional. They asked her to come home for a discussion. (When they were fresh-men in college thirty years before, college regulations would never have countenanced sexual relations between unmarried students.) The week-end was not a pleasant one—her mother spent it expressing her feelings of failure as a parent; her father remained silent and kept to himself.

Perhaps in hopes of influencing her, the family attended mass together on Sunday.

Doug, on the other hand, came from another background. His mother held unconventional views, belonged to no orthodox religion, and was open and accepting of Doug, his friends, and their lifestyles. Tracey was caught between her emotional involvement with Doug and the traditional sexual mores of her parents. Later she could see that she had been too intense and too dependent on Doug, wanting a permanent liaison rather than accepting the situation as it was. She devoted too much of herself to their relationship and too little to her academics. Doug, while reciprocating her feeling, was not ready for such a commitment. She struggled to find the right set of values for herself.

At the end of her first year at College A, Tracey transferred to another college in order to major in medical technology and because of the tension between her and Doug. The college was affiliated with a strongly conservative religious sect, and Tracey was only there a short time before she realized that the school was unsuitable for her and she dropped out. For the spring semester she returned to College A and Doug. At the end of another year of study, Tracey took a job assisting in a small clinic to find out if she wanted to make paramedicine her life's work. She held this job for one year. Deciding that she would not feel challenged or satisfied with work involved so much in the laboratory rather than with people, she resigned and enrolled in College C, where she planned to complete a major in biology and prepare for secondary school teaching.

During her first year at College C, she met Carl, a twenty-nine-year-old divorced man, father of twin daughters, aged four. Carl was the college librarian. She fell in love with him and in him she thought she had found someone with whom she could spend the rest of her life.

"The other night when we went to the movies, I kept falling asleep and I kept leaning over my chair and falling over on Carl, curling up with my head on his lap, and it just felt so good being that close to him, and I felt so good because he's this person that I know. I know the way he smells and I know the way he feels, and I know his muscles, I know what his balls are like—and I like that. It's just not me touching me, you know—but it's me touching someone else—and I care about that extension. I think a lot of young women, and even guys, they're very much into touching each other and holding each other and putting arms around each other, walking hand-in-hand. The physical aspect somehow seems to be some kind of release, or compensation, for the pressures that

people feel if they're alone—the pressures of middle-class America rip-
ping off the environment, the government becoming more fascistic, the
industries polluting the air. There's this cubistic landscape and it's very
harsh and it's very geometric, and then there are two people walking
down the street with their arms around each other and it just seems
somehow to be the only human way to react to such a thing, you know."

But Carl, like Doug, was not ready to enter into a long-term commitment. "Carl is afraid of love, he says things like, 'I don't want to feel
responsible for other people, I don't want them to feel responsible for me.
I just want to do what I want to do, I want them to do what they want
to do.' But I want more than that. I think there's more to love than that.
I am trying not to let my heart break—trying to accept the fact that
there's nothing there for me in the long-term sense."

In giving up Carl, Tracey realized she should not continue to live alone
in her own apartment and moved to a house rented by some students.
One of them, Duane, a recent dropout from a large university, began
pressing his interest on her rather vigorously. Eventually, and possibly
in her dejection over Carl, she had sex with Duane, but not without some
resentment toward him. "One morning when he came by my room, I was
impossible, really impossible, not a reasonable person at all. And it was
just because he was trying to get so close to me and I didn't want to be
idolized. He kept telling me how pretty I was and it just got me down.
This morning, I just pushed him out. I wish Carl had been there with
me instead. I'm glad Duane's going to Mexico next week."

This incident had occurred just before the end of the semester. Shortly
thereafter, Tracey realized she was not feeling well. She finally went to
a doctor who confirmed her worst fears—she was pregnant, and had an
infection, trichomoniasis, and possibly gonorrhea. Now, in addition to
the emotional upheaval she was experiencing, she had physical apprehensions. She reports that during this period she spent three weeks just
sitting in her room. "It was just everything—my general debilitated
physical state plus the fact that I felt as though no one else wanted to
know me, to touch me with their little finger even.

"Finally I got out and saw more people, I got out of the house. The
people in the house were depressing me. I got out to see what other
people were doing instead of sticking to myself with my own problems.
I also talked to other people about getting medical care from the state.
Now I've made up my mind to get an abortion. This I'll have to do on
my own. I can't call my family—I can't handle their confusion and

mine . . . it's my mistake and I have to deal with it . . . it's not their responsibility. I'm sure they'd be concerned."

The next time we saw Tracey she said she felt that her experiences had shaken her but also that she had been able to do a lot of thinking about herself and life in general.

"I think there is a certain validity in the traditional role. It has grounds, that's true. I think there's something else in there now, though, because of the acceptance of sexual freedom. I think it's really confusing for women right now to know what kind of an identity we have in this world today. Sexually when can we be responsive and warm and loving or angry and disgusted? There's so much pressure all around.

"I have some real questions about the lack of participation of the male in birth control. I mean that there should be a sharing of responsibilities and participation in the emotional end. At that time I really wanted someone who would drive me to the doctor's when I had to go to the doctor's, who would come up to the house when I didn't feel good.

"I have some new questions about what research shows up about polygamy and monogamy—I have some new questions about what research says about the emotional attachment of the female mind in comparison to the detachment of the male mind. Because right now those things are bugging the hell out of me. I'm very monogamous in my thinking and I've always only been with one person at a time, until this little thing in May and June this year. And obviously that's had some dramatic repercussions on my body and on my mind, and I don't like it and I don't want to do this polygamous sort of—here today and gone tomorrow way of doing things. And I don't think it's healthy, I don't think it's healthy for someone's mind because sex becomes a commodity, and the woman becomes a commodity, so to speak. On the other hand, moralizing about virginity just never entered my mind. If I love someone I was going to show it and I was going to be involved, and I sort of knew that from about the time I was six years old, and if I have to be honest—that's the way it's going to be.

"But I'm scared and I'm scared of the judgment thing—feelings that would come out that some people would think I am promiscuous . . . that would horrify me. I feel more comfortable with expressing myself than not expressing myself. And when I am with someone that I really like, then sex is very pleasurable, it's about one of the most lovable things I've known.

"But there are physical reasons for the traditional monogamous role, too, I can see now. I think it's probably a very negative thing for your body to be involved sexually with more than one person in a short period of time. The doctor said the same thing, too. The fact that sex is all internal for women—you know it's a nice warm hibernating place for bacteria—and leads to more infections—the chemical variance of people.

"Marriage binds two people too closely. I see it in my relationships with the opposite sex, I see it in my friends who are married. The wife should be able to relate to other men platonically and other women. In marriage, the world for women becomes very small and this happens to girls. They're insecure about relating with other people. Young women should also become involved with other women—because one of the things I found recently is that the only person who will feed you dinner and drive you around and love you when you're crying your eyes out is another woman. She knows because she's been through it, too.

"I haven't been too intellectually involved because I've always been so emotionally involved.

"I feel lucky now, though. Since the abortion I know that I can make choices now. I was lucky that I had a choice. Now I can work. There are really no restrictions—we can all do anything in this time in our life. I think I'll just live alone for a while. Passivity does not bring anything. You must make your own space in life. They don't move over for you—you have to make your own space."

This then, much of it in her own words, is the story of a young college woman who suffered emotional and physical pain because of her feminine orientation. She let things happen to her where a man would not. At the age when sexual desire is at its height, Tracey was a romantic. She was looking for a man to love and to cherish. She was also looking for a man because having left her sheltered home to go away to college, she needed someone to be a substitute for the absent family. She needed support. Although she appeared liberated in her dress and speech, inwardly she was still dependent. Her early relationships at college lacked awareness. She drifted into a caring-for and being-cared-for situation that gave her a lot of heartache because of its transiency. With more thoughtful consideration of her own feelings and motivations for going into these relationships, she would have been less vulnerable to pain and disappointment. She was too passive. She did not take command of her own life.

Tracey's family is still supporting her. When she does get her degree, it will not be before she is twenty-five. Her communication with her family is still not easy. But emotionally, she is moving toward a rapprochement. She wants to go home for a visit. It will be the first in three years.

The Anatomy of Sex

*S*EXUAL desire becomes strong in people after they undergo the physiological changes that occur at puberty, at about the age of twelve. Though this maturation occurs in everyone, our culture has been very secretive about sex and everything surrounding it—its anatomy, physiology, and role in life. Many women of college age are uninformed, and often misinformed about their own bodies. In order to acquaint you with reliable and straightforward information, we are quoting, with permission, part of a chapter from *The Student Guide to Sex on Campus* by The Student Committee on Human Sexuality (Yale University New York: The New American Library, Inc., 1971). This information in part is based upon the substantial recent research done by Masters and Johnson (*Human Sexual Response*[Boston: Little, Brown, and Co., 1970]).

Female Anatomy

The area between a woman's legs which constitutes her external sexual parts is called the *vulva*. The area covered with hair is called the *labia majora* and the folds of tissue which protrude around the opening to the vagina are called the *labia minora*. At their uppermost part the labia minora join to form a hood of skin over the structure called the *clitoris*. Usually not visible because it is covered by the skin hood, the clitoris is the female counterpart to the erectile part of the penis. The clitoris varies in size from that of a pea to about ¾ inch in length. If a woman spreads the labia minora apart and pulls back the clitoral hood, she is able to see the clitoris. Just beneath it is a small opening which leads to the urinary bladder. This opening is called the *urethra* and it, too, responds during the sexual response cycle. At the lower part of the vulva, and also at the entrance to the vagina on both sides, are glands called Bartholin's glands. They may become swollen from time to time or develop cysts. They are one of the areas that a doctor checks at the time of a pelvic examination. Ordinarily, they are not visible and cannot be felt. The labia majora, labia minora, and clitoris can be seen if a mirror is held between the legs.

Spreading the labia minora apart, it is possible to visualize the opening of the vagina and the ring of tissue around it—the *hymen*. The hymen, in reality, is not a separate tissue but simply a narrowed area between the vagina and the vulva, separating the vagina from the vulva. The tissue is about ½ inch in from the outside, contains small blood vessels which may bleed at the time of first intercourse, and is about ¹/₁₆ inch thick.

The *vagina* is the space beyond the hymen. It is a pouch within the body which, in reality, is a potential space, its walls being in touch with each other under ordinary circumstances. If a tampon is put into the vagina, then the vagina becomes the size of the tampon. If a penis is put into the vagina, the vagina becomes the size of the penis, or if a baby is coming through from the other direction, then the vagina adjusts itself to the size of the baby's head. The tissue lining the vagina is different from skin tissue; it is influenced by hormones produced in a woman's body and, like the mouth, contains different kinds of organisms (viruses, bacteria, yeast). A secretion is produced that protects women from infection. Both the vagina and the vulva contain nerves, blood vessels, and muscular tissue which enable them to respond at the time of sexual stimulation.

At the top of the vagina is the *cervix*. Cervix means neck, and the cervix is the neck of the womb; i.e., that part which extends out of the abdominal cavity and into the vagina. The cervix contains blood vessels and glands. The glands produce secretions throughout the menstrual cycle and are responsible for the mucus that many women notice about midway through this cycle.

A canal through the cervix leads to the cavity of the *womb* (more properly termed, the *uterus*). The cavity is called the endometrial cavity and is lined by the glands and blood vessels which are responsible for the

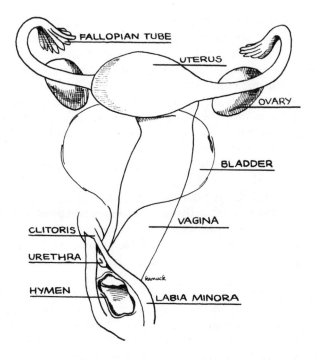

menstrual flow. Leading out of two corners of the endometrial cavity are the *Fallopian tubes.* The tubes carry the eggs each month from the ovary to the endometrium. Fertilization occurs in the tubes. The sperm go from the penis to the vagina up through the cervix and the endometrial cavity and into the tubes. If conception occurs, the egg then takes about six days to travel to the endometrial cavity and start growing within the endometrial lining. If the fertilized egg gets caught in the tubes (about once in every 200 pregnancies), this is known as a tubal or ectopic pregnancy, and it usually has to be removed by surgery. If pregnancy does not occur, then the egg travels to the uterus and is eventually discarded through the cervix. The egg is so small that it is not noticed in the regular fluid that comes out of a woman's vagina.

The *ovaries* are the female counterpart to the testicles. They produce eggs about the size of a speck of dust, usually at the rate of one a month. Most women in the course of a year will have a month when they don't release an egg. Some women will produce more than one egg—one of the ways in which twins and triplets are conceived. Occasionally, women may know when they are releasing an egg—either by an ache or pain in the lower part of the belly or by the increased mucus from the vagina or occasionally by slight bleeding midway between their regular periods. Occasionally the pain is severe and is known as "mittelschmerz." It may be severe enough to require medical help. At that time it is very important to let the doctor know when your period began so that an accurate diagnosis can be made. Fortunately, mittelschmerz is a condition which almost always can be treated with simple pain medication.

The ovaries also produce the hormones responsible for the menstrual cycle. Hormone levels are at their lowest when the menstrual flow begins. Soon after, a hormone called *estrogen* is produced as the ovary responds to a message from a center in the brain. The center is called the *pituitary,* and it in turn is under the influence of a higher center called the *hypothalamus.* No one is sure about all the factors which influence the hypothalamus but they include such things as diet, travel, exams, season of the year, anxiety, and general state of health. Thus, all of these factors may affect the ability of the hypothalamus to stimulate the pituitary to stimulate the ovary to produce the hormones. As stated above, soon after the beginning of the period, estrogen is produced. It builds up to a certain point (causing changes of its own in the lining of the uterus) at which time another signal from the pituitary causes an egg to be released. After the egg is released, a second hormone, *progesterone,* is produced. Both estrogen and progesterone continue to be produced until about five days before the period when their production stops, the levels in the body decrease, and the cycle starts all over again.

Many of a woman's bodily and emotional characteristics are influenced by estrogen and progesterone. The breasts enlarge as a result of the production of these hormones. The skin often clears with estrogen production but may develop acne when the progesterone production is highest. Many women retain fluid as a result of progesterone production. This leads to sensitivity of the breasts, bloating of the belly, and sometimes a change in bowel function (some women become constipated before their periods, while others develop diarrhea). Perhaps most important is the effect of estrogen in building up a protective lining in the vagina—especially important for women near the change of life (the menopause) when their ovaries cease to function. At that time, usually obvious because of a woman's emotional reactions and hot flashes (sudden short periods of feeling very warm and breaking into a sweat), it may

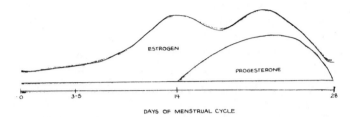

DAYS OF MENSTRUAL CYCLE

be very important to take estrogen pills in order to continue the protective effects of this hormone. Perhaps the most troublesome of the hormones' effects is the depression that many women experience before periods—an effect that can be treated by medication from a physician.

The time period during which the ovary produces estrogen, releases an egg, produces progesterone, and then stops for the menstrual flow is a span that varies greatly, especially among students. We have mentioned that diet, travel, anxiety, etc., can throw off the cycle. Indeed, we are told by our advisors that a very high percentage of students have very irregular periods which don't occur every twenty-eight days the way books say they should. A normal range, counting from the first day of one period to the first day of the next period, is between twenty-one and thirty-five days. About the only girl who can figure out when she is releasing an egg is the one who is very regular. Then, she should figure out when the next period is going to begin and count back fourteen days. Skipping a period is not unusual, especially in the summertime, and does not automatically signify pregnancy or indicate any serious hormonal problem.

Bleeding in between periods is abnormal unless it is the spotting at the time of ovulation. Periods usually last from three to seven days. Bleeding beyond seven days is a reason to see a doctor. Similarly, if no period has occurred for more than forty days, this is another reason to go to a physician to be examined and evaluated even if there is no possibility of pregnancy. The reason is that such a prolonged time between periods can mean that an egg was not released and that the lining of the uterus is becoming quite thickened. As a result, when a period does occur, it may be very heavy. The doctor could prevent such heavy bleeding by giving progesterone to bring on a more normal type of flow.

Male Anatomy

The *penis* and the *testicles* are the external male sexual organs. The penis is soft when a man is not sexually aroused and is erect when he is. A canal runs through it which can carry both sperm and urine, although not at the same time. That tube, as in the female, is called the *urethra*. The tip of the penis has a single urethral opening. The tissue at the head of the penis is similar to that of the clitoris. It is very sensitive and becomes engorged at the time of sexual arousal. Men who are circumcised do not have a hood of skin over the tip of the penis while those who have not had such an operation do have a hood similar to the clitoral hood. In the male, it is called the *foreskin*.

Two testicles, the male counterpart of the ovaries, lie in a sac called the *scrotum*. The scrotum hangs beneath the penis. One testicle is usually lower than the other. The testicles are sensitive to pressure and hurt if squeezed. Across the top of each testicle is a small structure which is called the *epididymis*. This leads from the testicle to the *ejaculatory duct,* a canal which eventually empties into the urethra. It is not unusual for a man to be able to feel a separate little lump on the testicle that represents the epididymis.

The testicles produce sperm, the male counterpart to the egg. Sperm production is influenced by many factors, perhaps the most important

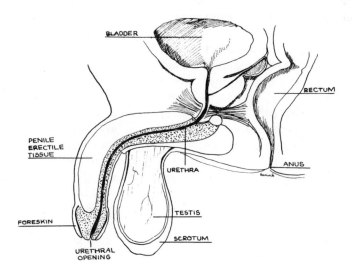

of which are heat and the general health. The common cold is often enough to reduce the sperm count below the normal levels of 20–100 million per twenty drops of fluid. In a single ejaculate (about a teaspoon of fluid), it is estimated there are about 500 million sperm. Glands which are adjacent to the ejaculatory duct, the passage from the epididymis to the urethra, produce the secretions that carry the sperm. These structures include the prostate, the seminal vesicles, and the Cowper's glands. *Ejaculation* is the release of the sperm-containing fluid from the genital tract. It may be brought about spontaneously during sleep—the so-called wet dream (nocturnal emission)—or as a result of masturbation, petting, or intercourse.

The testicles also produce androgens, the male hormone, as well as estrogens. Male hormone production is not believed to be cyclical as in the female, and there is no male counterpart to the female's menstrual flow. Androgens, the most influential of which is testosterone, cause development of male characteristics such as facial hair, chest hair, and deepened voice.

Sexual Intercourse

One widely used dictionary gives a definition of sexual intercourse which is somewhat misleading. After looking up different words such as coitus, cohabitation, and copulation, a student finally arrives at this definition: "Sexual intercourse is genital contact, especially insertion of penis into vagina followed by ejaculation." All students should be clear about the fact that you do not have to have ejaculation of the penis in the vagina to have intercourse, and simply placing the penis against the vulva does not constitute intercourse either. *Intercourse is the insertion of the penis into the vagina.* As mentioned earlier, at the time of first intercourse there may be some bleeding from the hymen since there are tiny blood vessels in the hymen which can break when the penis is inserted. But many women today use tampons or engage in sexual activity, such as fingering of the vagina, which leads to a stretching of the vaginal opening so that there is not necessarily any bleeding at the time of first intercourse. Thus, many women have stated that they have had no such bleeding. When there is bleeding it is similar to that of a nosebleed. The blood vessels are about the size of the blood vessels in the nose and the bleeding will stop fairly soon. If there is some bleeding at the time of first intercourse, then a period of abstinence for at least twenty-four hours should be observed. Also, at the time of first intercourse or soon after starting to have intercourse, it is not unusual to develop a bladder infection called cystitis. Cystitis may cause frequent urination, some blood within the urine, or burning on urination. These symptoms should be brought to a doctor's attention and treated as soon as possible. Cystitis is not difficult to treat but can be aggravated by continued sexual activity.

Sexual Response

The entire human body is able to respond sexually to many different types of stimuli. Odors, sights, sounds, touch—any of these may turn on the sex response system with which we are all born. Thanks to the research efforts of many investigators, most notably Masters and Johnson, we are now able to describe what happens to a human being when he or she is responding sexually.

Sexual response of genital structures as well as other areas of the body is essentially the same whether it be the result of autosexual (self-stimulation, masturbation), homosexual, or heterosexual stimulation. The type of response can be influenced by many factors including fatigue, health, drugs, stage of menstrual cycle, pregnancy, contraception; and, perhaps most important, the learning experiences (good and bad) which influence the way in which we respond to anything and everything.

There are many important differences between male and female response. However, in both sexes it is possible to describe stages of response, once again regardless of the stimulus or the social setting. These stages are called the excitement, plateau, orgasm, and resolution phases. In addition, in men, there is a stage after orgasm called the refractory period during which the man can't respond to any stimulus. The next paragraphs summarize current ideas, mostly from Masters and Johnson, about sexual response.

I. The Excitement Phase

The excitement phase in both sexes can be categorized by several general physiological changes as well as other changes that are specific to each sex. In both men and women, the pulse rate increases, blood pressure rises, contractions of voluntary and some involuntary muscles occur, and measles-like rash known as the "sex flush" may appear upon the skin. This sex flush can appear at almost any time in the sexual response cycle, or, as in many cases, it may fail to appear at all. If it does occur it is usually located in the area of the breasts and the upper abdomen. It is more common in women than in men.

The male's first response to sexual excitation is the erection and enlargement of the penis, which can take several seconds. Contrary to popular myth, the increased size of an erect penis is not in direct proportion to its size when flaccid. While a normally large penis may increase very little in length upon erection, a small one may double or triple its normal length. The result is that erect penises differ in size much less than do non-erect penises. In fact, the size of the penis is of very little importance to the enjoyment of intercourse.

Erection is due to the engorgement of the penis with blood (vasocongestion). Vasocongestion is essentially the most important of the physiological reactions to sexual stimuli, and it plays a significant role in both sexes.

Other changes in the male may include nipple erection, a tensing and thickening of the skin of the scrotum, which flattens the scrotum against the body, and a raising of the testes up into the sac resulting from a shortening of the cords from which the testes are suspended.

In the female, sexual arousal is initially signaled by a lubrication of the vagina. Regardless of the mode of arousal, the lubrication occurs within half a minute after the onset of effective stimulation. Contrary to earlier beliefs, the lubricating fluid does not originate in the uterus and travel downward through the cervix, nor does it arise from Bartholin's glands, the pair of glands located at the opening of the vagina. Although these glands do secrete several drops of fluid they are not responsible for the much larger amount of fluid found in the vagina during sexual excitement. The actual source of the lubricating fluid is a "sweating reaction" on the walls of the vagina.

At first glance, vaginal "sweating" and penile erection may seem to be unrelated responses, but in fact both are the result of vasocongestion. In the case of vaginal lubrication, the fluid apparently flows from blood vessels located in the tissues around the vagina when they are congested with blood.

It is not true (although it is commonly believed) that lubrication of the vagina indicates that a woman is fully aroused sexually. The moistening of the vaginal walls does make penetration of the penis possible (penetration before lubrication can range from difficult to painful), but before a woman is physiologically and psychologically prepared for the move toward orgasm, other bodily changes must occur.

Due to the location of very sensitive nerve endings within the clitoral glans, stimulation of the clitoris can increase a woman's level of sexual arousal. Nevertheless, this stimulation need not result from direct physical contact. Since the inner lips of the vagina are attached to a hood that covers the clitoris, the thrusting of the penis through the inner lips produces friction between the clitoris and the clitoral hood. The clitoris may also enlarge as a result of stimulation of the breasts or from purely psychological events such as erotic thoughts and sights.

Once stimulation has begun, the shaft of the clitoris increases in diameter, and the glans swells, due to vasocongestion. The degree of swelling, however great or small it may be, is not connected with the intensity of sexual responsiveness.

During stimulation the outer lips (major labia) of the vagina may open a bit from their normal position of contact at the vaginal midline. The inner lips (minor labia) may also swell as excitement mounts, and they may in fact contribute to the spreading apart of the outer lips.

As the labia are responding to stimulation, the vagina is changing from its normal state which resembles a collapsed cylinder. There is a gradual increase in diameter along the inner two-thirds of the vagina, accompanied by some slight lengthening of the cylinder. Engorgement of the blood vessels in the vaginal tissue takes place at the same time.

Relatively early in the excitement phase erection of the nipples of the female breasts occurs as a result of contracting muscle fibers. Vasocongestion produces an increased length and diameter in the nipples. Later in the excitement phase there is an increase in the size of the breasts and some swelling of the areolas (darker skin around the nipples).

II. Plateau Phase

The plateau phase is the second of the four divisions of the sexual response cycle, according to Masters and Johnson. Although it is not clearly separated from the excitement phase, which has already been described, there are some physiological conditions which help to delimit to some degree the plateau phase.

For both sexes, respiration, blood pressure, and pulse rate increase during the plateau phase. The sex flush may become more pronounced, or appear if it has not already done so. Muscle tension, both voluntary and involuntary, increases. The sphincter muscle, which holds the rec-

tum closed, may tighten or in fact be purposefully tightened by a participant as a means of increasing arousal.

For men the plateau phase begins when the erection of the penis is
complete. During this phase there are very few changes in penile size.
The testes, however, may increase in diameter to one and a half times
their normal unstimulated size. As this phase is nearing its end, the testes
attain full elevation, signaling the absolute imminence of orgasm. While
this is happening, the nipples may erect if they have not already done
so. If coitus is prolonged at this stage, several drops of a fluid, which is
not semen but that can contain some sperm cells, may emerge from the
Cowper's glands through the urethra (at the penile opening). Thus a
woman can be impregnated even if coitus interuptus is practiced, since
most males exhibit this phenomenon on at least some occasions.

Entrance into the plateau phase can be noted for females by such
changes as increased swelling of the areolas of the breasts as well as some
further nipple erection. Prolonged coitus in this phase may result in the
secretion of several drops of fluid from the Bartholin's glands.

The appearance of "the orgasmic platform" as described by Masters
and Johnson is the most dramatic female response during the plateau
phase. The engorgement and enlargement of the inner two-thirds of the
vagina that has been described as taking place during the excitement
phase continues, and now the tissues of the outer one-third of the vagina
become vasocongested, swell, and reduce the diameter of this area of the
vagina. Since the reduction is as much as 50 percent of the diameter of
this part of the vagina, the vagina actually tends to grip the penis,
providing a pleasurable addition to the other stimuli.

At about the same time as the appearance of the orgasmic platform,
the clitoris is elevated and retracted away from the vagina; its shaft
decreases by about one-half in length. The clitoris continues, however,
to respond to direct or approximate stimulation, including the thrusting
of the penis and manual manipulation. It should be noted, however, that
at this point direct physical manipulation of the clitoris (after retraction
has occurred) may be painful, whereas manipulation of the parts of the
body nearby (vagina, inner and outer lips) may serve to stimulate the
clitoris in an indirect and pleasurable fashion.

Engorgement of blood vessels (vasocongestion) and increased muscle
tension are the main physiological bases of the plateau phase. In fact,
vasocongestion accounts for a color change in the inner lips at the end
of this stage, signaling the imminence of orgasm in the female.

III. Orgasmic Phase

Many bodily changes occur in both men and women during orgasm. Respiration, blood pressure, and pulse rate achieve their peak values at this stage of the sexual response cycle. The sex flush is most prominent at this point, and muscles such as those in the neck, legs, arms, buttocks, and abdomen may contract spasmodically. The muscles of the hands and feet may contract quite strongly, often resulting in a tight gripping of the partner during orgasm.

The basic component of the female orgasm is a rhythmic series of muscular contractions of the outer third of the vagina—the orgasmic platform. The initial contractions occur at intervals of four-fifths of a second, and the later ones occur at increasing intervals with decreasing intensity. The number of contractions in an orgasm may range from around three (a mild orgasm) to about ten or twelve (an intense orgasm) or even higher in a few cases. As the outer third of the vagina is undergoing contractions, the uterus undergoes contractions similar to but milder than those of labor prior to childbirth.

The primary component of the male orgasm is a rhythmic series of contractions in the penis, occurring initially at intervals of four-fifths of a second and tapering off to longer intervals and reduced intensity as time passes. These contractions power the ejaculation of the male's semen, which is accomplished in two stages. The first stage develops as follows: fluid containing sperm emanates from the testes and flows into sacs known as seminal vesicles and ampullae. This fluid is then forced into the urethra by contractions of these structures, while at the same time a fluid from the prostate is being expelled by contractions into the urethra. These fluids are all received at the base of the penis in a bulb in the urethra that enlarges several times to accept them. At this point, the subjective experience of orgasm occurs.

The second stage of the male orgasm begins with a series of rhythmical contractions of the fluid-containing bulb in the urethra and contractions of the penis itself, which together force the semen outward under pressure great enough to carry it perhaps two feet if unobstructed.

During orgasm the vasocongestion that has been built up throughout the body subsides with the release of the congested blood to the rest of the body. The muscular tension that has peaked is released in a series of spasms throughout the body that may result in the forceful grasping of the partner. At this point the resolution phase begins.

IV. Resolution Phase

For women the first signs of this fourth and final phase are decreased engorgement of the areolas and the disappearance of the sex flush, if it has been present. Next, a fine layer of perspiration may develop, often ranging from the neck to the thighs, including the palms of the hands and the soles of the feet. Some men also exhibit this sweating phenomenon, but usually it is confined to the hands and feet in males. In the case of either sex, however, the degree of sweating is not connected with the amount of physical effort exhibited during orgasm.

Several seconds after orgasm, the clitoris returns to its normal position; after several minutes or more, it returns to its normal size. As these changes proceed, the inner area of the vagina begins to shrink. The female body is usually completely returned to its normally unstimulated condition within one-half to three-fourths of an hour, although this stage may take several hours.

For men the loss of erection is the first sign of the resolution stage. The penis shrinks rapidly at first, but the final stage of diminishing size may occur more slowly. The male's scrotum, testes, and nipples return to their unstimulated state, and the sex flush disappears. In both sexes, the end of the resolution stage is marked by the return to normal levels of respiration, pulse rate, and blood pressure.

Once orgasm has occurred, the male experiences what is termed a "refractory period" during which he cannot become sexually aroused. The refractory period may be as short as a few minutes, but it usually lasts much longer, perhaps twenty minutes or more. (At age seventy, it may last a week.) The penis may be congested and erect at this stage; however, orgasm is not yet possible.

According to Masters and Johnson, women do not have the same post-orgasmic experience as men. They can remain in a sexually aroused state, which contrasts with the male's refractory period. From this state it is possible, with continued effective stimulation, to experience subsequent orgasms. More typically, a woman's orgasm is followed by a prolonged resolution stage during which sexual tension gradually decreases.

The above description of the four phases of the sexual response cycle should not be interpreted as being representative of a typical sexual experience. Just as people exhibit individual differences, each sexual experience may have characteristics of its own that do not exactly fit into the average description presented. These additional, or perhaps omitted, characteristics should not be considered a detriment to the sexual experience; individual variations are quite often to one's advantage in the sense of increased sexual pleasure.

It should be especially noted that the description of the sexual response cycle presented here applies to any form of sexual experience. It is not at all peculiar to male-female coitus. Masturbation, homosexual stimulation, fondling of the breasts, manipulation of the genitals by a partner, as well as sexual intercourse, all lead to essentially the same series of responses. Of course, the psychological reactions to and the pleasure achieved from these different types of experience should be expected to be quite different. Some will be pleasant and some distasteful. Nevertheless, the physiological responses are not different.

14

Contraception, Pregnancy, and VD

IT is during the teens and twenties that women are most fertile, and yet there is a considerable amount of misinformation held by them about the biological facts of pregnancy and fertility. Despite the pill, considered to be an important factor in the sexual revolution, and in use now for about fifteen years, rates for premarital pregnancy and abortions, as well as venereal disease, have increased each year for those under twenty. Sociologists estimate that one bride out of five is pregnant on her wedding day. Four percent of all unmarried eighteen-year-old white women in the United States have been pregnant at least once; this is 12 percent of those who are sexually active, according to the Commission on Population Growth and the American Future. There is evidence, moreover, that premarital intercourse is beginning at younger ages and the extent is increasing among teenagers, according to a recent report published in *Family Planning Perspectives* on "The Sexual Experience of Young Unmarried Women in the United States."

Young women, whether they are sexually active or not, should be informed about the physiology of sex and contraception just as they should know about the effects of drugs or nutrition. The maturity of the young woman having sex can be determined, in part at least, by the provision she makes for contraception. Ruth and Harrup Freeman, who did research on college seniors and sex, reported that while college women respect both virginity and nonvirginity in others, pregnancy is not condemned as immoral, but as stupid and incautious. Young people often take chances, little realizing that it is only necessary to have sex once to become pregnant. Agencies that give contraceptive counsel and contraceptive materials include Planned Parenthood, the county health services, the family doctor, and often the college health service. For those young women who lack information about contraception, what to do if they become pregnant or contract a disease, the more essential information follows.

Contraception

Contraception refers to methods used to prevent pregnancy. Not all methods have the same degree of efficiency. Nevertheless, any method is superior to no method. The ratings below indicate the effectiveness of contraceptive methods. They are based on the results of four recent studies of the failure rates of the various methods. The numbers were designated by the authors and have no significance except to indicate the relative effectiveness of the methods. The higher the rating number, the higher the risk of pregnancy. Absolute security against pregnancy is to have no intercourse, and hence that has a rating of zero. Naturally the highest risk (20) is having sexual intercourse without using any form of contraception.

Risk of Pregnancy With Various Contraceptives

Method of Contraception	Risk Rating
No sexual intercourse	0
Sterilization of female by tying the fallopian tubes (tubal ligation)	1
Sterilization of male by tying the vas deferens (vasectomy)	1.5
Hormonal birth control pills	2
Condom used with jelly, foam, or cream	2.5
Intra-uterine device (IUD)	3
Condom	3.5
Diaphragm with jelly or cream	3.5
Vaginal spermicides (foam, jelly, cream)	5
Rhythm	9
Coitus interruptus (withdrawal)	9
No contraceptive device	20*

*Highest risk, not effective

These methods of contraception are explained below. Methods offering temporary protection against pregnancy and hence most often used by young people are described first. Sterilization is considered last as it is almost always permanent and not encouraged for young people who have not had any children.

Hormonal birth control pill (the pill); used by the woman.

How it works: The pill is made up of chemical hormones of estrogen and progesterone, which cause the woman's body to act as it would if it were actually pregnant. These hormones prevent the egg from being released from the ovary. If there is no egg to be fertilized, there can be no pregnancy. Menstruation continues but periods decrease in amount and duration. The pill must be taken for a specified number of days. At present, pills taken less often (monthly or yearly) are being tested and may be in use by the time this book is published.

Effectiveness and duration: Most effective temporary contraception method at present if taken precisely as directed. The pill and the IUD are the contraceptives most commonly used by women under thirty. Protection lasts as long as the pill is taken exactly as prescribed. If three or more pills are missed, separately or consecutively, another form of contraception should be used during that month and birth control pills continued also.

How obtained: From a doctor by prescription. A physical examination and regular checkups are customary. Some women, because of certain physical conditions, should not use the pill.

Intrauterine device (IUD); used by the woman.

How it works: The IUD is a device, usually made of plastic or metal, that comes in a number of shapes. It is inserted into the uterus and remains there indefinitely or until removed. Because of its presence in the uterus, the egg does not become fertilized. The specific reason for this is not understood at the present time.

Effectiveness and duration: Highly effective and gives protection for as long as the IUD remains in the uterus.

How obtained: From a physician and inserted by a physician.

Condom (also called prophylactics or rubbers); used by the man.

How it works: The condom is made of latex or animal gut shaped like the finger of a rubber glove. The man places it over the erect penis just before inserting it into the woman's vagina. Since the sperm are ejaculated into the condom they are prevented from entering the vagina and fertilizing the egg if one is present in the uterus or in the fallopian tubes.

Effectiveness and duration: The condom is as effective as the diaphragm. It has the advantage of a high degree of protection against venereal disease. It is the only contraceptive that does. If the woman uses a spermicidal foam and the man uses a condom, it has almost 100% effectiveness. Protection lasts for one intercourse.

How obtained: Condoms can be purchased in any drugstore without a prescription.

Diaphragm; used by the woman.

How it works: The diaphragm is a shallow cuplike device made of thin rubber with a firm outer rim. It is inserted into the vagina to cover the cervix prior to intercourse and is not removed for six to eight hours after intercourse. It is used with spermicidal jelly. It is two ways effective: by blocking the sperm from entering the uterus and by killing the sperm with the jelly if they should get by the blockade.

Effectiveness and duration: Very good. Prior to the discovery of the pill it was the most commonly used form of contraception by women. To be effective spermicidal jelly, cream or foam must be added for each further act of sexual intercourse.

How obtained: From a doctor. Diaphragms come in different sizes and must be fitted to individual measurements.

Vaginal spermicides; used by the woman.

How they work: Vaginal spermicides come in a variety of forms: creams, jellies, foams, and foaming suppositories. They are usually sold with a special applicator. The spermicide is inserted into the vagina at the cervix. It sets up a chemical barrier which kills the sperm that reach it and blocks the cervix so that sperm cannot enter.

Effectiveness and duration: Quite effective; when used in conjunction with a condom they have high effectiveness. Foam is considered more reliable, as jellies do not always cover the entire area. Must be inserted according to directions, usually from thirty to sixty minutes prior to intercourse with repeated applications for each sexual act.

How obtained: Can be purchased in any drug store without a prescription.

Rhythm; used by both partners and based on the fertility period during the woman's cycle.

How it works: Pregnancy occurs only during ovulation, that is, the time of the month when the egg is released from the ovary. If a woman refrains from having sexual intercourse during the period just before, during, and just after ovulating, she will not become pregnant since there will be no egg present for the sperm to fertilize. Ovulation usually, but not always, occurs in the middle of the menstrual cycle. Women having a regular 28-day period would be most fertile on day 14. By not having sexual intercourse from day 10 to day 18, this fertile period would be avoided.

Effectiveness and duration: Considered to have low reliability because of the difficulty in knowing exactly when ovulation occurs. Even with consistently regular periods ovulation may change due to physical or psychological causes. In order to be effective, expert professional guidance is needed. Protection lasts as long as sexual relations are avoided during the period of ovulation.

How obtained: By seeing a gynecologist and working out the safe period through the use of month-to-month records of the menstrual period and by taking the body temperature.

Coitus Interruptus (withdrawal); used by the man.

How it works: The man withdraws his penis from the woman's vagina before he ejaculates the semen which contain the sperm.

Effectiveness and duration: Not considered very effective for the following reasons: some semen may be released before the man withdraws and without his knowledge and the first semen has the highest concentration of sperm. Semen that is ejaculated around the woman's genitals may get inside and swim up to the uterus or the fallopian tubes where an egg may be present for fertilization. The man must have good self-control and timing to withdraw at the proper time. Neither partner experiences as much satisfaction as with other, less demanding, forms of contraception. Protection lasts as long as effective withdrawal is practiced and semen is not released to unite with an egg.

How obtained: Through the self-control of the sexual partners.

Tubal ligation; sterilization by tying the fallopian tubes in the woman.

How it works: An operation is performed on the woman, either through the abdominal wall or the vagina, which involves cutting, removing a segment, and tying the fallopian tubes. Hence the egg from the ovary cannot be carried to the uterus and is instead absorbed by the woman's body. Tubes can also be closed through the use of heat or chemicals. A new ten-minute procedure involves minimum abdominal surgery and hospitalization. It is effected by the injection of a fluid to locate the ends of the fallopian tubes and then cauterizing them.

Effectiveness and duration: Very effective. Sterilization is permanent under present methods. Reversing the operation has not proved too successful.

How obtained: Through the services of a gynecologist or surgeon in a hospital using an anesthetic.

Vasectomy; sterilization by tying the vas deferens in the man.

How it works: The vas deferens are tubes which carry the sperm from the testes to the urethra, located in the penis. The tube is cut and tied so that the sperm are blocked from entering the semen. Sexual functioning remains the same, but pregnancy cannot occur.

Effectiveness and duration: Very effective. Sterilization is usually permanent. Reversing the operation is possible but not often effective.

How obtained: Can be performed in a doctor's office by a urologist, a surgeon, or a general practitioner under a local anesthetic. It is considered a minor operation.

Douching

Douching is not considered an effective method of contraception for a douche can reach only sperm that are in the vagina, and may actually force them into the uterus. A gynecologist once wrote that no woman

can run as fast to douche as sperm can swim up into the fallopian
tubes.

Morning-after pill

The morning-after pill is not a method of contraception but rather a
complicated procedure of preventing pregnancy if the possibility occurs.
The morning-after pill, to be effective, must be taken within a short time,
one to three days after intercourse. It consists of a large amount of
estrogen and can be obtained only by prescription. It may cause vomiting
and nausea. Not all people can take the morning-after pill because of
certain physical conditions: e.g., hepatitis, heart trouble, blood clots, and
so forth. In December 1972 it was attacked by Ralph Nader's Research
Group as a health hazard as it contains Diethylstilbestrol (DES) which
may increase the risk of cancer in women with a family history of breast
or genital cancer.

Pregnancy

Pregnancy occurs during ovulation, the time when the egg or ovum
is released by the ovary and travels down the fallopian tube into the
uterus. In theory, ovulation usually occurs during the middle of the
menstrual cycle. In a woman having regular twenty-eight-day periods,
for example, ovulation would take place two weeks after the first day of
her period. Pregnancy is effected when the egg is fertilized by the sperm,
usually in the fallopian tube but sometimes in the uterus. When fertilized,
the egg travels to the uterus and becomes attached to the wall of the
uterus. If unfertilized, it is discharged from the body during menstruation. The least fertile time is just before, during, and after the menstrual
period. However, some women have become pregnant at this time.

How do you know if you are pregnant?

The first indication is usually a missed period. But nothing about sex
seems to have categorical answers, so even the cessation, or the appearance, of the period is not an infallible sign. Periods are missed for other
physical reasons, and psychological ones also; and women have been
known to menstruate even though pregnant. Other signs are tender and
enlarged breasts and morning nausea. Morning sickness, however, is not
inevitable; or it may appear at other times during the day as well. For
a more reliable diagnosis, a pregnancy test is recommended. This is a test

of a sample of the urine, which, if positive, will contain hormones not present otherwise. The recommended time to have the test is two weeks following the first missed period or forty-two days after the first day of the last menstrual period. If it is negative and a regular period doesn't begin within two weeks, another test should be run. It is important not to delay having the pregnancy test so that, if positive, whatever future course is taken, there will be enough time for planning and action.

If you find that you have an unintended or unwanted pregnancy, these are the alternatives that are available to you:

—You may have an abortion
—You may marry and have the child
—You may have the child, remain single, and rear the child yourself
—You may have the child and give it up for adoption

No matter what course you decide to follow, you will experience some emotional distress. Before taking final action, we strongly advise you to seek pregnancy counseling. You will receive reputable referrals and sympathetic help. Your experience may have genuine learning results. For such counseling, contact Planned Parenthood, your college's health service, or if these agencies are not available, ask your doctor or call the social services department of a hospital. These agencies can give you information about abortions, pre-and postnatal care, maternity homes, and adoption agencies.

Abortion has become increasingly accepted in the United States as a means of terminating unwanted or problem pregnancies. An abortion during the first three months of pregnancy is legal in all states; for one performed during the third to the seventh month of pregnancy, a state may regulate the medical aspects. The laws therefore may vary from state to state. The states may apply severe restrictions on requests for abortions following the twenty-sixth week of pregnancy. (Ruling of the U.S. Supreme Court, January 22, 1973).

Some communities list *Abortion Information* in the Index of the yellow pages of the telephone directory; a few use billboard posters to give telephone numbers. The timing of having an abortion is highly important, so do not wait. The reason for this is that an abortion performed in the first twelve weeks of pregnancy is a simple procedure and is usually done on an outpatient basis. Abortion procedures after the thirteenth week are more complicated and require hospitalization.

Early abortions are effected at the present time mainly by dilation and curettage, called D and C. A dilation and curettage is usually performed under a local anesthetic, and the abortion occurs after dilation of the cervix by either a tube inserted into the uterus which removes the tissue by suction vacuum or by a small instrument called a curette which scoops out the fetal tissue. When the pregnancy is of longer duration, a method called a hysterotomy is necessary. This is similar to a caesarean delivery and requires an operation upon the outside of the lower abdomen and removal of the fetal tissue by surgery. Also, future pregnancies will have to be delivered by caesarean section. This is, of course, a more complicated procedure, and is consequently more expensive and takes more time. Another method used for late abortion is called amniocentesis or "salting out" and is accomplished by drawing out the amniotic fluid surrounding the fetus and then replacing it with a saline solution. This brings about uterine contractions which expel the nonliving fetus within a period of twelve to forty-eight hours.

Abortion is a method of terminating unwanted and accidental pregnancies. It is not a method of contraception. Complications may develop, and the expense, the discomfort, and the health hazards are greater than with regular methods of contraception. Abortions cost anywhere from nothing if handled through welfare services to $100 and up. The fee depends upon the length of pregnancy, the method used, the availability of treatment, and so forth.

Not all women take the option of terminating an unwanted pregnancy by abortion; some decide to have the baby. If you get married, having a child will cause major changes in your and your husband's plans for the future—such as interfering with your education, in addition to assuming the responsibilities of parenthood. Statistically, your marriage will have less chance of enduring. According to the Census Bureau's analysis of marriage and divorce, released in October 1971, twice as many divorces occur in marriages where the man is under twenty-two and the woman under twenty than in couples over these ages. The birth of a child within the first two years of married life also doubles the chance of a divorce, perhaps because a high proportion of these children are the result of premarital or unwanted pregnancies.

You may decide to have your baby and keep it or give it up for adoption. There are agencies that offer care and assistance to women during this period and information may be obtained from the same agencies that furnish abortion information. If you wish to put your child up for adoption, early counseling is advisable, since this decision is usually irrevocable. It is an emotional wrench for a woman to bear a child and then to give it up, and she should have as much help as possible in sorting out and evaluating her feelings. Adoption agencies are sometimes listed in the yellow pages of the telephone directory. Most adoptions are now handled through the social services department of the county. Among other adoption agencies are the Catholic Social Service, the Jewish Family Service Agency, and the Florence Crittenden Association. These agencies offer counseling services or can refer you to such help.

Married or not, there are women who make good mothers and who want children. These women are usually mature and psychologically secure. Often they have successful careers. Some are married in all respects except the legal one. This kind of person can give a child a good healthy environment and enjoy the satisfactions of motherhood. To assist single parents, there are agencies such as the Family Service Association (private) or public social service organizations. With the greater number of unmarried women in public prominence having children, there is bound to be an increase in the public's acceptance and assistance.

Why would you, or any college woman for that matter, get pregnant when you don't want to despite the availability of contraceptive information? The reasons are many. You may not want to face up to the fact that you would consider premarital sex, and rather than take precautions, you just let it happen. You may have conflicting and ambiguous emotions regarding your beliefs and the code you want to support, and contraception means thinking about it and taking a stand. It also requires planning and precise action. You may invite illegitimate pregnancy because of hostility toward your parents, or in order to avoid facing other problems, such as failing grades. You may take chances and act on impulse rather than face reality because you think it can't happen to you. You may use pregnancy to get your man, or you may consider it unromantic to take premeditated precautions.

Of course, there are times when women become pregnant because the contraceptives they are using fail. Also, some women may be ignorant of contraceptives and/or how conception occurs. On the other hand, a woman may be motivated consciously or unconsciously to become pregnant. Pamela Lowry, in an article in the *Harvard Crimson* in August 1971, pointed out that when this occurs she must then face up to parenthood—which may not have been included in the fantasy. In a study done by Ramshaw and Bruyn at Cowell Hospital at the University of California, it was found that women are more apt to get pregnant during transition periods such as moving, changing contraceptive methods, or changing boyfriends. One writer emphasized that our culture socializes women to be romantic. Women feel obliged to react as though they were rushed off their feet and overcome with passion, and that being prepared does not fit this image. Women are not free to accept their sexuality as men do.

Men, too, can be responsible for encouraging carelessness with contraceptives and taking risks during sex. Some men who have underlying feelings of sexual inadequacy may try to prove their virility to themselves by conceiving a child. When sex is used to validate one's identity, woman or man, it is an avoidance of facing reality, similar to the cop-out of drug use. Moreover, it is belittling; a person has more than a sexual identity. Mature people have additional facets to their personality which add interest to their sexual dimension.

Venereal Disease

One of the unfortunate by-products of the sexual revolution and the pill has been the increase in venereal disease. In the state of California, for example, the number of reported cases of gonorrhea increased by 15,000 from 1969 to 1970. One-fifth of these cases involved teen-age girls and boys. There are unknown numbers of unreported cases. Unless treated in the early stages, these diseases can be destructive. "Syphilis can cause brain damage, heart disease, blindness and congenital deformities, while gonorrhea can lead to sterility, arthritis, and a variety of lesser ailments," according to the *New York Times* of April 5, 1972.

When venereal disease occurs, it is a signal that either you or the man you are having sex with has been involved with someone else. VD is highly contagious and is contracted by having intercourse with someone who has it. It is the hazard of having casual sex with many partners and can be contracted through either heterosexual or homosexual intercourse.

Syphilis is a blood-borne disease which enters the system through small breaks in the skin. It is a disease of stages. The first stage appears from nine days to three months after exposure and is usually a small sore in the genital area which may not hurt at all. In the woman, the sore may be on the cervix and may therefore go unnoticed. If it is untreated, the sore will disappear, although the germs remain present. In the second stage, a rash appears on part or all of the body, and that, too disappears in time. The germs then lie dormant in the body for five, ten, twenty, or more years. Eventually they manifest themselves by attacking the heart or the nervous system, causing paralysis or death. Women who have syphilis and bear children can infect them during the gestation period through the placenta, often giving birth to stillborn or blind children.

Gonorrhea is difficult to detect in a woman who has contracted it because, unlike a man, she may have no symptoms. She may not know she has it unless her male partner tells her he has it or has contracted it. In the man, it is evidenced by severe burning during urination and a thick yellow discharge. The woman may have similar but milder symptoms or may only find out months later, when the gonorrhea germs have ascended to the uterus and to the tubes. She may then have lower abdominal pain, recurring pelvic infections, and above-normal temperatures. Sterility can result because the tubes become closed. If a woman infected with gonorrhea does become pregnant, she may infect the child while it is passing through the birth canal. In 1971 gonorrhea was the number one communicable disease, according to the *New York Times* report cited previously.

Treated early, venereal diseases are easily cured; it is when the germs become entrenched that treatment is more difficult.

There is some evidence linking early sexual intercourse, or intercourse with many partners, to cervical cancer. This has not been proved, nor has the cause been determined. A recent study at Baylor College of Medicine in Texas of 10,000 teenage girls, all of whom were sexually experienced, revealed that 23 out of 1,000 had abnormal cells in the cervical lining compared to 12 out of 1,000 women of all ages in the population. Abnormal cells do not mean that cancer is present, but indicate that there is a predisposition to cancer. It would be advisable for people who have sex with many partners to have a blood test once a year. To allay the fears of teenagers, doctors are not required to inform parents of minors who have contracted venereal disease.

Men have long had tacit approval for premarital sex; and society is moving, more rapidly in some groups and in some parts of the country than in others, toward accepting the same mores for women. Since women become pregnant and men do not, and since venereal disease in women is more difficult to detect than in men, sex can have more complex implications for them. Women should be aware, therefore, of the possible consequences and safeguard themselves against them.

This chapter is included because many young women do not have accurate knowledge of contraceptives or of what to do should they become pregnant. It is not meant to encourage sexual intercourse. Determining what is right and when it is right is part of achieving one's identity and an integral part of the enjoyment of sex.

5

Getting High

IT was a large room, unlighted except for a desk lamp. As the first rays of the sun colored the sky outside, the black shadows in the room began to gray. Ellen was sitting on a large window seat looking out. Barely visible in the distance were the deserted quadrangle and the clock tower of the library. The sepulchral whiteness of the new administration building was visible even in the predawn light. Ellen's reverie was interrupted by the chimes of the clock. It was 6:00 A.M. She turned and looked into the room. Littered with coke bottles and plastic cups, cigarette butts floating in their dregs, it was a mess. Clothes, books, and personal articles were everywhere in helter-skelter fashion. She could hear the echo of her mother's comments on her last visit. Sometime soon she would clean it up.

In one corner of the room, Jennifer was still huddled holding on to herself. Her long hair in disarray fell over her face hiding it. She had been sitting, facing that corner with her back to the room, for more than seven hours; and for seven hours Ellen and anyone who came by to help had gently, patiently, soothingly, tried to talk Jennifer down. Jennifer had appeared the previous night about eleven o'clock in a terrified state, and rushed into the corner. She was at turns, incoherent, almost violent, talkative, and weeping. She had freaked out on mescaline. Her fear of the unknown, of death and of life, were so real it frightened some of her friends who were trying to help her. There had been some tense moments, but Ellen was confident that they could cope with the situation. The task required patience. She knew now that they would make it but she was very tired and she had an eight o'clock class. Jackie had been a welcome sight when she came in an hour or so earlier to take over. Finally, Jackie's soft mocking voice said something that triggered Jennifer's release. Jennifer talked to them rationally for a few minutes and then went to her room to sleep.

It's hard to understand why Jennifer went into such heavy drug use. She said it was peer group influence and curiosity.

Why do some people take drugs? Ghetto residents are said to take drugs because they are boxed into a dreary, bleak, poverty-prone life with no hope of breaking out. Most middle-class college students never know an hour of such an existence.

Students who were asked why they took their first drug gave the following responses: Being persuaded to try it in a social situation, curiosity, for "kicks," wanting to have greater understanding of themselves, not wanting to be left out, showing that they have independence, and so forth. The pressures of the peer group are evidently the most important influence for trying drugs. There is apparently a zealous fervor about "turning on" one's friends. The commonly held belief of the evil drug pusher inveigling young people into a life of drugs is just not valid.

Researchers at the University of Michigan believe there are two reasons why people take drugs for the first time. One is the availability of the drug, the other is the amount of pressure put on the person to start taking drugs. Students report that they use marijuana for social reasons, because it gives them a pleasant feeling, it produces camaraderie and admits them to a group. Marijuana is a kind of "social" drug in college groups used the way the older generation uses alcohol.

There are no statistics on the use of illegal drugs that are considered accurate, but surveys taken of student use are the most plentiful. These indicate that college students, by and large, favor alcohol and tobacco along with marijuana. Other drugs are used, but to a lesser extent. Despite the illegal status of marijuana, its use has become almost respectable in college circles. The first Gallup poll of college students' use was made in 1967 when 5 percent said they had experimented with marijuana. In 1972 more than half of the college-student population (51 percent) had used it. During the same period, use of hallucinogens rose from 1 to 18 percent. (This figure probably refers to the LSD-type drugs.) Some students, like Jennifer, are introduced to drugs in college; others learn about them earlier. The trend for experimenting with drugs progresses downward through the age groups; what began in colleges in the sixties is now in the junior high school and even in lower grades. A *New York Times* article of January 10, 1972 reported that drug use was one of the most urgent school problems of the seventies. The article reported an increasing use of alcohol, cigarettes, marijuana, LSD, barbiturates and amphetamines from grades 7 to 12. Only glue sniffing showed a decline—fortunately, as it is considered to be one of the most damaging substances to the liver. It also has a deleterious effect on the kidneys and the central nervous system. Marijuana use ranged from 9 percent in grade 7 to 26 percent in grade 12.

In San Mateo County, California, where surveys of drug use by junior and senior high school students have been made yearly since 1968, alcohol tops marijuana in regular use. In 1973 almost 29 percent of the senior girls and 40 percent of the senior boys admitted drinking alcoholic beverages 50 times or more during the previous year; marijuana was smoked 50 times or more by 20 percent of the senior girls and 32 percent of the senior boys. The statistics for tobacco use, 50 times or more, are higher for the girls at 32 percent than for the boys at 30 percent. The figures in the study have shown a yearly increase; only barbiturate and amphetamine use showed a downward trend in 1972 and 1973. All studies report a higher incidence of drug use by males than by females.

A survey on the use of drugs by students at the University of California at Berkeley in 1971 indicated that marijuana had a slight edge over alcohol for regular use. The percentages of students who were using drugs are shown in table 8.

8. UNIVERSITY STUDENTS' USE OF DRUGS*		
Type of Drug	Used at Least Once	Occasional to Regular Use
Marijuana	75.2%	51.3%
Alcohol	79.4	47.2
Psychedelics	30.6	8.2
Amphetamines	53.2	6.8
Downers	19.8	3.6
Cocaine	10.7	2.5
Heroin	3.0	.7

*These figures were produced by student members of a Special Chancellor's Committee on Drug Abuse from a completed questionnaire survey of 924 fellow students who represented a cross-section of the university.

The highest drug use is said to be among youth on the west coast, then the east, next the midwest, with the least among the youth in the south. Some people who study the use of drugs contend, however, that this is the route that drugs take, rather than where the action is. What's popular in the west merely takes a while to reach the south.

What kind of people are the students who use drugs? Are drug users different from average students? If so, how are they different?

Generally, moderate marijuana users are no different from nonusers. Almost always they began their drug use with alcohol and tobacco. The moderate drug user, according to Blum *et. al.,* is described as flexible, interested in parties, sex, and pleasure. The authors note, however, that many students are concerned about the effects of drugs and are swayed from the use of the more dangerous drugs through drug education in the schools. Notwithstanding, some experts believe that drugs have become linked with growing up for young people and have become part of their life-style.

In "Patterns of Drug Usage Among University Students: IV. Use of Marihuana, Amphetamines, Opium, and LSD by Undergraduates," Drs. Doris H. Milman and Jeffrey L. Anker found that students who used these drugs had other characteristics which non-drug users were not as prone to have. (See *Journal of the American College Health Association* 20 [1971], 96 –105.) They found users of illicit drugs were more often also tobacco smokers and alcohol drinkers to intoxication. A higher percentage were men. Both women and men were more likely to be single than married, but living with a partner of the opposite sex or having sexual experiences. Women who dated were more apt to smoke marijuana than women who did not date, perhaps illustrating the peer group influence. Moreover, drug users' friends were generally drug users as well. As measured by their fathers' income and education, as a group they were usually of a higher social class than nonusers. Nonetheless, their relationships with their parents were more often classified as "worsening." Students with "excellent" parental relationships used drugs on a less-than-average basis, while those with "good" relationships had an average prevalence of illicit drug use. Also, drug users were more liable to psychiatric difficulties and to negative moods. The heaviest users were usually also venders of drugs.

The authors found a negative relationship between drug use and regular church attendance and married status; i.e., students who attended church regularly and students who were married were less likely to use drugs; they found no relationship between drug usage and academic standing. The study was done at ten undergraduate campuses on the east coast and was based on over six thousand responses from students.

Psychologists believe that those who become drug abusers, contrasted to the average person, are less able to manage their frustrations, feel insecure in their strivings for maturity and have trouble relating to others. These failures in personal relationships apparently build up tensions and anxieties that are then replaced with drug-induced feelings of euphoria and self-confidence. Unfortunately, dealing with problems by changing one's feelings chemically does not alter the problems. It is counterproductive because it is a palliative measure only and blocks any real and permanent resolution of a difficulty.

Anyone who takes drugs is aware of the psychological and/or physical dependence* and tolerance properties of drugs. Psychological dependence refers to a drive or craving which requires periodic and continued use of the drug to produce satisfaction or to avoid discomfort, or to get a good feeling, usually euphoria. Physical dependence is based on a biochemical change in the body of the user from the drug, so that it is normal only when the drug is present. Increasing amounts are needed to maintain the drug's effects on the body. Tolerance to a drug refers to the adaptation of the body cells so that they become able to function normally in the presence of the drug. Tolerance, however, keeps rising so that it is necessary to increase the amount of the drug taken to achieve the same feeling—which is the case in practically all drugs, legal and illegal, except marijuana.

Upon discontinuance of the drug, the addicted person's bodily equilibrium is upset and physical reactions, known as withdrawal symptoms, occur. These may be mild, such as yawning, headaches, sleeplessness, or they may be severe, such as excruciating pains, vomiting, coma, and even death. The heroin addict, for example, will appear to have all the symptoms of a cold when the drug is beginning to wear off. Later the symptoms become more severe—shakes, chills, muscle cramps, sharp pains in the abdomen, and excessive sweating. Withdrawal symptoms from alcohol and barbiturate addiction are even more severe. Table 9 shows the effects of habit-forming drugs.

*In 1965 the World Health Organization Expert Committee on Addiction Producing Drugs recommended that the term *drug dependence* be used instead of *drug addiction* to cover all kinds of drug abuse.

9. SOME EFFECTS OF HABIT-FORMING DRUGS*			
Name of Drug	Psychological Dependence	Physical Dependence [Withdrawal sickness?]	Tolerance [Are increasing doses needed for same effect?]
Heroin	strong	yes	yes
Barbiturates	strong	yes	yes
Alcohol	strong	yes	yes
Cocaine	strong	no	yes
Amphetamine	strong	no	yes
Caffeine	mild	no	yes
Marijuana	moderate	no	no
Nicotine	strong	no	yes
LSD	strong	no	yes

Source: *The New York Times*, April 22, 1972, p. 37.

*Compiled from data of Drs. Maurice Seevers of Ann Arbor, Michigan, and Joel Fort of San Francisco, California.

Habituation to drugs is only one of the risks of drug use. Drug dependence robs a person of her freedom, but also causes her psychological damage, and often physical damage to her liver, kidneys, and brain. Death from hemorrhages in the esophagus from cirrhosis of the liver is a pretty unpleasant way to die, but life in the bondage of the unreal world of drugs, without personal accomplishments or satisfactions is a pretty unpleasant way to live.

One of the misconceptions that people have is that drugs causing physical dependence are more dangerous than drugs that are only psychologically, but not physically, addictive. This, of course, is not true. Physical withdrawal may be severely uncomfortable and even dangerous, but it is usually accomplished in a matter of days, or a week or so. It is the psychological hold that the drug maintains over the individual that is the critical factor in overcoming the habit. Psychological dependence, moreover, is continually reinforced and fortified by physical dependence. Hence overcoming drug dependence is easier in the earlier stages. Some people claim to have become dependent on drugs through prescription by a doctor. This seldom happens. Millions of patients receive morphine in hospitals but only a small fraction ever want to take the drug again. Moreover, people begin taking drugs in most cases, not for the treatment of a physical ailment, but because of social pressures.

One of the pitfalls of drug use is disinhibition. Drugs reduce tension and increase relaxation to the point where the user no longer exerts control over herself. In a sexual encounter, for example, a woman using drugs, most commonly alcohol, may not be in a position to determine whether she is a mutual partner in a loving act or an object being used sexually.

It is only recently that drugs have been the subject of research and there are still many unknowns. One of these unknowns is the effect of alcohol and other drugs on brain cells. Some scientists believe that drugs impair the intricate functioning of the brain and may kill brain cells. Unlike other nerve cells in the body, brain cells cannot rejuvenate. Once gone, they are gone forever. Another unknown is the effect of drugs on the offspring of users. Obstetricians have increasingly become aware of the dangers of drugs, and of maternal illness, on the embryo during the first trimester of pregnancy. Even aspirin, long considered a safe drug, has recently come under suspicion.

Jennifer's Trip

HE scene given in the opening paragraphs of Chapter 15 describes an experience of a college student, Jennifer, age twenty. She is a thoughtful young woman who talked about her experiences with searching honesty. She offered to be interviewed about her drug experience to illustrate some of the problems faced by young women going away to college. This is an actual case history; only names and places have been changed for purposes of anonymity.

Jennifer can offer no specific reason for her heavy drug use except that she wanted to find out about herself. She suffered through a period of identity confusion (given in Chapter 10) but not all young people who have identity problems turn to drugs. Jennifer's second year in college was spent in depression and deep introspection. She emerged from that year with a strong commitment to prepare herself for work in one of the helping professions.

Jennifer comes from a middle-class family; both parents are college educated. She attended a small high school where she was unaware of any drug use, and there was no drug education. Upon high school graduation, Jennifer went to a small women's college in the Midwest.

The interview follows.

JENNIFER: That was the beginning of . . . that was my first taste of freedom. First time I ever lived away from home for any extended period of time and I loved it. I didn't know what to do with myself. I wanted to do everything. There were so many things that I wanted to get into that I couldn't even be bothered with the academics. Because I was in the process of trying to find out who I was as a person and that was taking up all my time. And as a result I neglected my academic work. I got involved in drugs. . . .

I did all my drugs, all my heavy drug doing was done my first year in college.

INTERVIEWER: How did you start?

J: Curiosity. Peer group influence. Those are the two major things. . . . I started out smoking grass. And from there I went to hash. And from there I went to mescaline. On my first mescaline trip, I freaked out.

I: How did you freak out, tell me about it.

J: I was in a dorm mate's room, I was in her room with her and I was feeling very euphoric and just beautiful like I was . . . I felt like I was very much in tune with this person, I was a part of her almost. I felt what she felt without saying anything. Just as I picked up on her vibes and she picked up on mine something started happening. She started remembering an acid experience that she had, taking LSD . . . brought back connection in her memory . . . that she had been on acid and flipping out, it was a heavy acid trip that she took and somebody tried to flip her, that was the purpose of the trip—that she would possibly blow her mind, somebody wanted to do her in, and make her flip out on acid.

I: She wasn't on a trip?

J: No, she was straight, I was the one who was tripping and it freaked both of us out, freaked her out that I was picking up on it and that she was feeling it, freaked me out that perhaps I thought I'd caused it because I was tripping. And we both became almost estranged because of that. Because we had both gotten into so much of what each other was doing, we walked down the hall to another friend's, a mutual friend of ours— Ellen—went into her room, went to opposite ends of the room and both crawled into corners. She crawled under a table into a corner and I just crawled into a corner and stayed in that corner for about eight hours . . . I didn't move for eight hours. I was very scared and for some reason I couldn't handle space. In the corner, except for my back, there just was no space to handle. I was still tripping when I came out of the corner but I was coming down.

I: Did anybody try to help you?

J: Oh yes, there were a lot of people there trying to help me. Friends tried to help by talking me down. When a person flips out and flips up and away and their head just kind of spins out and goes somewhere—they leave reality totally, they are completely out of touch; the precarious hold they had on reality while they were tripping is gone. They've lost it. They've completely lost their sense of time and surroundings and everything.

You talk them back down to earth. And there were numerous people doing that to me, taking turns when they got tired. And finally something that somebody said just . . . brought me right down. Somebody said some crazy thing on purpose . . . spaghetti has roots and it grows in Italy. . . . And I said, No, that's not right. And I came right down.

While I was up I can remember crying, and I can remember people holding me, trying to pull me out of the corner and holding me, and sometimes . . . crying and sometimes crawling back into the corner, not wanting . . . I can remember wanting to be touched and held and needing to be touched and held, and not wanting to be touched at all. I didn't want anybody to touch me. I had no concept of time, to this day.

A guy had sent me roses before that . . . beautiful flowers . . . and while I was tripping in the corner I was thinking those roses were dying, which they were of course; and I kept saying My roses are dying My roses are dying and I wanted to die also while I was tripping. During part of that trip I felt a desire to die, my death wish. . . . I was banging my head against the wall, very hard, and not feeling it. Not feeling the pain. Somebody put their hand up in front of my forehead, I didn't know there was a hand there, it felt no different from the wall. . . . Which is how far I had become removed from my body, in physical sensation, when I got into wanting to smash my head against the wall. I was not feeling pain.

I: So did you give up psychedelics then?

J: No. From there I got into acid. Lot of acid during spring, my freshman year. When I tripped it was more of a nature trip . . . because it was spring. Oh, I can remember walking down to the center of town and we had kind of like a park in the middle which is a grassy thing and we had a monument, a statue of some . . . and the pigeons did their thing on him you know, people threw eggs on him occasionally; a few benches and trees and they had tulip bulbs that erupted in the springtime through the ground, and I can remember going down there . . . and we were there so early in the morning, that the worms were still out in the grass. And we were lying down and digging these worms in the grass. And it was very cool and the sunlight hadn't started to warm things yet really, and the worms were just out there sunning themselves, catching the few rays that weren't strong enough yet to dry them up. And we were just digging all these worms in the grass, and gradually as it got later they all crawled away, went back into the sod. It was nice . . . down there talking to the worms . . . it was pretty strange, too.

We had been up all night, we were tripping all night. We dropped acid at about oh maybe nine o'clock at night, it must have been later, maybe it was around eleven at night, went straight through the night tripping. And . . . naturally waited up to see the dawn. That was one of my most beautiful experiences. My more beautiful experience on acid was watching the sun come up. I can remember sitting on a sundeck, and watching . . . it's very hard for me to explain, except the feelings that I had during it were very powerful, I don't even know if I can find the right words to explain what I was feeling now when I think back on it.

It was black and dark and I remember looking at the outline of the trees and they had no leaves on them yet, they were just like skeletons of trees, and they were black and the sky was blue-black. And the dawn started to come and birds, you know, started their twittering and waking-up thing. And gradually as more light came into the sky and into the world around me the trees, I remember being very much into the trees, changed from just silhouettes of black or blue-black and took on dimension, they took on form, they became trees. As it got lighter I could see they had a color of their own. They were grey, or they were black and they were brown and they had you know scaly trunks and their bark was different, whereas before they'd just been outlines. They were two-dimensional, like on a piece of paper, and as the light came they took on form and shape, became a tree. And then the sunlight was something else, the colors were just incredibly beautiful. That was one of my better trips, watching the sun rise, the dawn.

I: Do you have the feeling or desire to do it again?

J: No. No. Not now.

I: Did you ever?

J: Since I stopped, no. I have no desire now. Whether I will in the future, I can't say . . .

I don't feel the necessity or the desire to do any sort of hallucinogenic drug . . .

I: Did you try any other drugs?

J: Mm. I did, once, a mixture of cocaine and something else. I think it was heroin. It was in a capsule and it was specifically for medical use.

It was given to people who were in intense pain in that it just knocked them out, just took them so far away from their pain . . . people who were dying from cancer or something.

I: Did you have any physical reactions to the drugs?

J: Oh, specifically acid. All drugs, but mostly acid. I stopped when I realized pretty much what I was doing to me when I was taking drugs. I started realizing after taking acid for a while that I was missing some things, that I'd had, that I didn't have anymore. That I seemed to be losing, like my memory. My memory seemed to have kind of gotten shot full of holes. And I didn't remember some things that I had previously remembered, had more difficulty remembering things. My memory was just getting superweak. And also my level of paranoia was distorted and out of proportion. When you're tripping you're paranoid anyway. One of the things about the drug that's very common is a feeling that everybody knows you're tripping and everybody's after you because you're tripping, not really after you but it's a paranoia . . .

All looking at you and all saying to each other, every word everybody's saying is she's tripping or he's tripping or . . . I know those people are tripping . . . or something like this . . . And it's so unreal but it's very real for the person who's tripping . . . very much a part of the trip is always this underlying . . . "everybody's watching me as if I'm some sort of a strange animal" and I found after doing acid for a while that this lingered after I was straight. I still was paranoid.

Still you know little things that wouldn't have bothered me were just blown out of proportion and became big and unreal monsters. This got to me and started bothering me.

Also because I just stopped wanting to give a masochistic trip to my body. Doing it in, you know. Filling it full of whatever unnatural substance I could find.

I: Why do you think you started?

J: I think part of it was masochistic. Part of it was curiosity, part of it was peer influence, curiosity I mean, wanting to find great revelations. Looking for answers to problems that I had, through acid . . .

I: Well how did you come to stop taking drugs?

J: Initially it happened through a person who informed me very bluntly—a guy—that what I was doing to myself was . . . fucking up my body. Fucking up my head. Giving myself an all-round bad time, doing myself in. This is going to do nothing in the long run but mess you up. Scramble your brain. And I listened because things being what they were, falling into perspective and time, I was right to listen. I was ready. It was almost as if in my kharma this was this person's cue to come onstage, give me his spiel, that was his place in my life, was to do this for me. And I was right to listen to him. He was a local guy who'd been into drugs, especially acid. He'd also done a lot of cocaine. But then he kicked it.

From what I gathered he did it for himself. It was a self-awareness that made him not want to do it anymore. Wanting to be someplace else than where he was . . . changing of his own accord. Some people such as heroin addicts need help in all this because besides being psychologically addicted they are very much . . . their bodies are addicted—they need it . . . it's very traumatic for them not to have it, they go through withdrawals and things like that which they may die from, which is a reality.

It comes mostly I think from the person stopping and taking stock of what they're doing and whether it's worth it to them, whether . . . there is a gain for them in it all. Or whether in reality it's an escape and a copout. They're doing it so they will not have to look at themselves as people. I think it comes from wanting to get to know yourself. You can't do this when you're on drugs, really. There's too much artificial happening inside your body, and your mind, for you to carry on a good communication with yourself. Real communication with yourself. Because it's artificial and stimulating and it won't be real when you're straight again, because you'll be on a completely different plane, than you were before.

I don't think if somebody could prove to me that it would just make me an incredibly great person if I went out and started doing acid again, they showed me all these facts and statistics and said, judging from how much acid you've done . . . and if you started taking drugs again it would . . . a whole new insight on the world and all these different aspects, I'd probably say yeah, Go away. I have no desire to do it again, at this point.

17

Drugs and Their Effects

FROM prehistoric times, alcohol and other drugs have been used the world over for religious, social, and medical reasons. In the present time, drugs are proliferating at such a rapid pace it is estimated that in ten years there may be one hundred times the number of psychoactive substances than are available today. This proliferation presages a continuing drug problem. We live in a drug-oriented society. We turn on our television sets for fifteen minutes and learn that we get instant relief from headaches, stomachaches, nervous tension, and emotional upsets, to say nothing of backaches, muscle spasms, and congested nasal passages, by taking a pill. Some people take pills for kicks.

Experts agree that many important basic facts are not known about drug usage and there is disagreement about the significance of what is known. One of the factors which contribute to differences of opinion is that psychoactive substances affect the complicated performances of the brain, but scientists still have little understanding of the biochemistry of the brain. No young person today is free from contact with drugs, including alcohol and tobacco, which are available to her. Whether she makes use of them or not, she should be informed of their existence and their effects on the user.

Some drugs seem harmless; others are known to be lethal. With virtually all drugs, however, the more taken, the greater the risk and the less likely there is to be a beneficial or pleasurable effect. In addition to alcohol, the drugs discussed in this chapter are some of the drugs regulated by the Federal Comprehensive Drug Abuse Prevention and Control Act of 1970. The use of them without prescription carries fines, and for repeated offenses, jail terms. In addition to the possibility of forfeiting one's personal freedom and civil liberties, a conviction can be a liability in seeking future employment or professional licensing. Alcohol, while not illegal, is causing consternation because of its increasing use and abuse. For the sake of brevity, and because of the extended coverage given to the hazards of nicotine use for the past ten to twenty years, tobacco is not discussed in this section.

Marijuana

Marijuana is one of the oldest drugs known to man. It has been used for thousands of years in most countries of the world for religious and medical purposes. It is produced from the common hemp plant, *cannabis sativa,* used in the manufacture of rope. It grows wild in temperate climates, including North America. Also produced from this plant, but of considerably greater strength, are charas from India and hashish from the Middle East and North Africa. The potency of *cannabis sativa* depends upon the soil and climate where it is grown and upon the part of the plant used in making the drug. Potent forms of the drug are produced from the resin secreted from the flowering tops of the female plant. Weaker substances are derived from the leaves, stems, and flowering shoots of the plant. Decreasing progressively in strength from the potent charas and hashish are ganja, bhang, and marijuana, which is the weakest.

Tetrahydrocannabinol (THC) is the active ingredient in marijuana. It has been produced synthetically and since it can be produced in specific strengths, it is now possible to do controlled experiments of its effects on animals and humans.

In general, marijuana produces euphoria and relaxation and is mildly analgesic. It is three times stronger when smoked than when taken orally. Physical effects accompanying the use of marijuana include reddening of the eyes, although the pupils do not change in size, increased heartbeat, itching and tingling sensations of the skin, and dryness of the mouth and throat. Some persons may experience gastrointestinal upsets resulting in nausea, vomiting, and diarrhea. Also reported are blurred vision, impaired hand steadiness, muscle weakness, and sleepiness. No heightening of sensory awareness can be detected by objective tests. Although noncaloric in itself, marijuana gives some people large appetites, especially for sweets.

As with alcohol and other drugs, the psychological effects on the user are influenced by her personality, mood, and the situation, in addition to the amount taken or smoked. To achieve the desired results, one must learn how to smoke it, to recognize the effects and how to prolong them. Reported subjective effects include euphoria, uncontrollable laughter, mental confusion and flight of ideas, slowed time sense, difficulty in making decisions, dreamlike states, impaired short-term memory, and the lessening of aggressive tendencies. In high doses, marijuana can cause hallucinations. Although initially the smoker may become more friendly, she becomes less so with the passage of time. Heavy use by students would interfere with their work since experiments indicate that marijuana impairs reading comprehension and interferes with judgment and intellectual functions.

Alcohol, tobacco, and marijuana are the most commonly used drugs in college circles. Just as previous generations were introduced to smoking, the present generation learns about marijuana. Most researchers, while still not completely aware of the effects of marijuana, and especially the long-term effects, do not believe that marijuana is as dangerous a drug as it was publicized to be by the Federal Bureau of Narcotics in the 1930s. It does not produce the toxic reactions observed with high doses of alcohol, amphetamines, barbiturates, and many other drugs. No lasting ill effects and no fatalities have been reported.

The National Commission on Marijuana and Dangerous Drugs released a report in March 1973 based on an eighteen-month study which recommended decriminalization for possession of the drug for personal use. Production and distribution commercially would remain criminal activities. No legal action has been taken on this report.

At the present time marijuana is not used medically in the United States, although prior to 1937 it was used in treating a variety of illnesses. Experimental use shows some positive results in the treatment of glaucoma. In other countries, over the centuries, it has been prescribed for a variety of ailments from headaches to tetanus.

Marijuana is not physically addictive and is considered to have low to moderate potential for psychological dependence. It has what appears to be "reverse tolerance," that is, regular users are more sensitive than the newly initiated, needing only a small amount to achieve a psychoactive effect.

Alcohol

Alcohol was probably discovered by accident in prehistoric times when the nomadic tribes settled on the land and became agriculturalists. The basic substance in alcoholic beverages is ethanol or ethyl alcohol. It is derived from sugar-containing agricultural products that are fermented by yeast. Also used are starch-containing products that can be converted into fermentable sugar. Alcoholic beverages may be made from grains, fruits, berries, cactuses, flowers, tree saps, milk, and honey.

The abuse of alcohol by some proportion of the population has accompanied its use since recorded history. People for whom alcohol is a problem are called alcoholics. An alcoholic is defined as a person who has lost control over her drinking; i.e., she cannot have one or two drinks and stop; and who uses alcoholic beverages to the extent that it harms her medically and socially. Although the majority of people can handle this psychoactive substance, about 10 percent of the adult American population cannot. There are now believed to be over nine million alcoholics in the United States. Moreover, the alcoholic does not suffer alone. At least four persons, usually family members, are deleteriously affected by one alcoholic, according to Alcoholics Anonymous. Hence the number of Americans affected by alcohol is much greater than the 10 percent who are alcoholics. Alcohol has claimed a far higher percentage of abusers than other drugs because it is legal, accessible, and pushed. It is also socially acceptable in most circles.

There is no specific stereotype of the alcoholic. Psychologists studying the emotional and personal characteristics of the problem drinker believe that the alcoholic tends to be immature and unable to accept frustration, depression, and anxiety. Society, however, and the particular culture are contributing factors, too. Some researchers believe alcoholism is learned behavior; others support the view that a genetic factor is involved. One researcher in human development reported that the woman alcoholic, as a teenager, will have been depressed, self-negating, and distrustful. Another says that the younger woman drinks to relieve anxiety, the older woman because of depression. Women are also believed to start drinking heavily due to a specific cause such as an unresolved conflict in their lives or because of a period of boredom or loneliness. Whatever the cause, the woman who needs more and more drinks to achieve a desired effect, and who drinks in order to cope, or to obviate coping, is an alcoholic, incipient or actual.

Although a depressant, in low doses alcohol acts as a stimulant because of its disinhibiting effect (hence the sound which rises from the cocktail party), but with increasing amounts, its depressant action comes into play. Alcohol is absorbed into the blood at the rate of approximately one drink per hour, so that the intensity of the effects can be lessened by drinking slowly. Initially, alcohol may produce a pleasant euphoric effect. It relieves tensions and anxieties and there is a lessening of inhibitions. With increased consumption the physical effects of alcohol intoxication become noticeable; i.e., unsteady gait, slurred speech, tiredness, sleepiness, and eventually stupor. There is a decrease in intellectual and motor ability and in sensory perception. Judgment is impaired. Changes in emotions may produce crying, laughing, shouting, or anger. Excessive amounts of alcohol over months or years cause brain damage and damage to the heart and liver. A high concentration of alcohol in the blood is believed to decrease the amount of oxygen to the neurons, causing them to cease functioning and to die. When alcoholic consumption at any given time is too large more areas of the brain become depressed, eventually causing coma and death. As noted later in discussing barbiturates, alcohol taken in conjunction with barbiturates is dangerous because the depressing action on the central nervous system of each drug is exaggerated when both drugs are taken together. The chronic abuse of alcohol decreases the life span by ten or twelve years. Alcoholism ranks fourth as a cause of death in the United States, mainly from cirrhosis of the liver.

As with other addictive drugs, curing alcoholism is easier in the early stages and may also prevent permanent physical damage to the organs of the body that are susceptible. Although a drink may seem to make it easier to face a problem, the habitual use of alcohol as a coping mechanism will stunt a person's psychological and social growth. Hence the younger a woman turns to alcohol, the more difficult it is for her to break the habit. Alcohol is physically and psychologically addictive. Tolerance occurs and withdrawal symptoms are severe.

Depressants (Sedatives-Hypnotics)

Drugs in this category depress the central nervous system (the brain and spinal cord); minor doses have a calming effect and produce drowsiness and sleep. Depressants are made up of a variety of drugs and include sedative-hypnotics (sleeping pills), tranquilizers, barbiturates, and alcohol, discussed previously. Among the most widely used of the barbiturates are Nembutal, Seconal, and Phenobarbital; other sedative-hypnotics include Miltown or Equinal, Doriden, Valium, Quaalude, and chloral hydrate. Pills in these categories are sometimes referred to as "downers."

Depressants are used medically to treat anxiety, insomnia, high blood pressure, hyperthyroidism, and are used before surgery. Barbiturates were first manufactured from barbituric acid in 1903; today there are more than fifty brands dispensed by pharmacists. The barbiturates are the most common of the sleeping pills and the most abused. The comments which follow will center upon them. They are obtainable legally only by prescription and are used in cases where sleep and relaxation are necessary. Taken in large quantities, they produce symptoms of alcohol intoxication such as euphoria, slurring of speech, confusion, drowsiness, disinhibition, alteration of time perception, staggering, loss of balance, falling, quick temper, and a quarrelsome disposition. Accidental overdoses can result because the person becomes confused and does not remember how many pills have been taken. When consumed in conjunction with alcohol, they are particularly dangerous because their joint effect is stronger than either drug alone.

Like many other drugs, barbiturates are suspected of causing brain damage. Furthermore, barbiturates are dangerous because tolerance develops quickly but the lethal dose remains the same. Withdrawal from barbiturates is severe, and can be life-threatening—even more so than narcotic withdrawal.

The potential for physical and psychological dependence of depressants is high. A case history as told by the mother of a young woman addicted to barbiturates is given in Chapter 18.

Stimulants

Although natural stimulants have been known from earliest times (tea drinking reputedly dates back to 2700 B.C.), synthetic stimulants are a more recent arrival within the last fifty years. The more commonly known and used synthetic stimulants are the amphetamines (Benzedrine and Dexedrine) and the similar drug, methamphetamine ("speed"). Stimulants are mood elevators; on a short-term basis they speed up energy, confidence, alertness, and well-being. With heavy long-term use, this activity turns into repetitive or compulsive behavior. Like other drugs, these effects result from the influence of the stimulant drug on the central nervous system which reverses fatigue, stimulates respiration, and depresses appetite.

Stimulants are used legally for depression, narcolepsy, and weight control. Their efficacy in weight loss and in treating depression is questionable, however, which has brought their use for these purposes under serious question. They have also been used effectively in treating hyperkinetic children where the drug has the opposite effect—that of reducing activity.

Illegally, amphetamines are taken in large amounts intravenously to produce an exalted euphoria, a "high." This rush, similar to the reaction from heroin, is followed by depression, often very severe. Chronic abusers suffer from malnutrition and paranoid psychosis. Their behavior is often unstable and violent. Shooting amphetamines is more common among hard drug users and rare in college circles. College students may use amphetamines occasionally to keep awake, to accomplish a big job, or to get the energy for a cramming session. Athletes and truck drivers have been known to use them to improve their performance or to stay awake for long periods, hence the name, "Pep Pill." Legal production of amphetamines has been cut back severely in order to control their diversion into illicit channels.

Tolerance occurs rapidly and hence the amount taken keeps increasing and is difficult to stabilize. The long-term organic damage to the body from these drugs is not known at present.

Cocaine is a natural stimulant with effects similar to the amphetamines but of shorter duration. It is derived from the coca plant grown in Peru primarily, but also in other parts of South America. It was introduced to Europeans during the mid-nineteenth century as a local anesthetic and as a cure for morphine addiction. Once it became obvious that abuse of cocaine often resulted, its use medicinally was limited to specific local (surface) anesthesia, primarily by eye, ear, nose, and throat specialists. Cocaine is described as a feeling-suppressant, analgesic, and stimulating drug. Initially it produces euphoria, and later, irritability, excitement and delusional states.

It is a drug that is more often sniffed than injected, which can cause irreversible impairment of the septum. It is not considered physically addictive, i.e., producing tolerance and withdrawal symptoms. It is considered a high-risk drug in that a greater proportion of people who use cocaine become abusers than would occur with a drug such as alcohol.

Hallucinogens-Psychedelics (LSD-type)

Hallucinogens-psychedelics are a collection of drugs which can produce hallucinations: i.e., auditory or visual perceptions without any external object or stimulus. Often sounds are experienced visually and colors are sensed aurally. The effects are unpredictable and the user may be unable to distinguish between what is real and what is imagined. Users may become disoriented, and judgments of one's actions may be completely incorrect.

Hallucinogens can be natural or synthetic. Perhaps the best known of the natural drugs is mescaline derived from the buttons of the peyote cactus plant grown in Mexico and Cuba. Synthetic hallucinogens are many, including LSD (lysergic acid diethylamide) and DOM, more popularly known as STP. DOM is said to be two hundred times more potent than peyote, LSD is about ten times more powerful than DOM. It is not feasible to discuss all of the synthetic hallucinogens here, so the following comments will be limited to LSD. The effects of other hallucinogens and psychedelic drugs are similar.

LSD is taken orally and produces physical changes that include dilated pupils, increased pulse and heart rates, tremors, elevated blood pressure, chills, increased body temperature, flushing, pallor, irregular appetite, and urgency of urination.

Time passes slowly and some users assert they have religiouslike experiences giving them insights into themselves and nature. The effects may not disappear completely. One subject reported a good trip when she saw the clothes in her closet dancing to Bach, her plants reaching out to welcome her, but on a bad trip she envisioned herself as an onion which, layer by layer, was being destroyed. She believed that death would come with the stripping of the final layer, and for eight hours she sat crouched in terror, with her body enfolded in her arms, holding on to her life. Flashbacks of the hallucination occurred for the next ten or twelve months, bringing with them the fear and panic she originally experienced.

Some medical authorities report that among the adverse reactions from chronic use of LSD are what appears to be basic personality changes which may result in the subjects dropping out of society. They believe that the ability to think and concentrate is impaired to a degree which makes functioning in the mainstream of life difficult.

Information regarding the effect of hallucinogen-type drugs on the brain and the body is meager, but LSD seems to be an erratic substance.

Hallucinogens-psychedelics are not physically addictive, but as with all drugs, the risk of drug abuse with its physical and psychological damage is always present. Tolerance is common with most of these drugs. With LSD tolerance develops quickly if taken for several days in succession, but disappears after a period of abstinence.

Heroin

The principal natural narcotic drugs come from the opium poppy, a plant grown originally in Asia Minor. This plant produces opium, morphine, heroin, and codeine, all of which have a high potential for psychological and physical dependence. Heroin, a derivative of opium, is a dangerous narcotic, not so much because of the effect of the drug on the body, but because of the physical and psychological side effects and because it is against the law and our existing social policy criminalizes its use. Although morphine and codeine are used medically, heroin is not.

After a dose, the user may experience a high and a temporary feeling of self confidence and relaxation; physical and emotional troubles evaporate. Mentally the user slows down, brain activity is decreased, and the person becomes disinterested, indifferent, and unfeeling. She will sit around just nodding out. Tolerance to the drug happens quickly, leading to larger and larger doses. Since heroin is illegal and expensive, and the craving for it so strong, the user's energies are no longer directed toward school and the normal activities of youth, but are wholly concentrated on obtaining the drug and the money to pay for it. When the drug begins to wear off, the addict has a wide range of symptoms, from enlarging eye pupils which were formerly pinpoints, to cold symptoms, to severe pains and feelings of nervousness and desperation. The drug's euphoric qualities disappear with use, but now the addict needs the drug to remain normal. Dependency has taken over her life—she is no longer free and may never be again.

Although physical dependence on heroin can be overcome in a matter of days, or at most a week or so, psychological dependence is extremely difficult to conquer. Tolerance occurs rapidly.

To sum up, from the information available, we know that the effects of drugs differ with different individuals. Each person at a party taking pills, smoking hash, or drinking alcohol, will have different reactions depending upon her personality, the amount that is taken, her physical condition, her psychological set, what she expects from the drug, whether she is in a friendly social situation, etc. Drug abusers agree that a paranoia develops with illicit drug taking; that they feel they are being watched, followed, or talked about. Other consequences, such as the drug's permanent effects on the body and on brain cells, are still unknown. But enough is known to make it clear that drug experimentation is risky.

A Mother's Trauma over a Downhead

HE following is a story of a drug user as told by her mother. The drugs used were depressants, or downers, but the behavior is similar to that of alcoholics. The material presented in this case history is an actual taping of a conversation between the mother and one of the authors. Names and places have been changed for anonymity.

Marian, in her early forties, is an articulate woman. She had a certain indefinable presence in addition to an attractive appearance and a quick, intelligent manner. She is the mother of three children, the oldest a boy, and two younger girls. Joan, the older daughter, became a drug addict at nineteen.

Marian's husband, Bob, is vice-president of an electronics firm. During the early years of their marriage, while Marian's husband was scaling the executive ladder, the family moved often. Marian said that with each advancement the company moved him to a new location. When their children were in high school (the oldest a senior and the youngest in junior high) her husband was made vice-president and was moved from Atlanta to the west coast. The family purchased a home in an exclusive suburb. In the new community drugs were a part of the high school scene, although Marian had not at first been aware of it.

INTERVIEWER: How did you feel when you found out that Joan was on drugs?

MARIAN: Numb, I just felt numb. She was away at college and came

home for a weekend. She said to me: "I have something to tell
you . . . I tried some cocaine in school last week." Then she said, "I'm
sorry and I don't want to do it again." I couldn't reply. What do you
say? Then she went off with some of her friends. Now I think she was
trying to tell me something else, too. She was warning me. . . .

I was in the kitchen preparing the dinner, pondering on this when
things started to fall into place. Each weekend she came home she'd been
loose as a goose—she said they had a wine party for someone's twenty-
first birthday, or a party to start the weekend. But can wine make you
that groggy? Maybe they drank a lot more than was implied. I know it
makes me sleepy but not like that. . . . Maybe in great quantity it
can . . . kept running through my mind. What else could it be? I didn't
know then that the kids were taking pills. I knew nothing; I had no
background to refer to. I knew of course there was stuff called Seconal
or Nembutal but the only thing I knew about it at that point was that
they gave it to you in the hospital to go to sleep at night. I hadn't even
heard rumors that kids took stuff like that for kicks.

Well, I didn't have long to wonder. Susan, my younger daughter who
is seventeen, came into the kitchen then and asked me what was the
matter. And I told her.

She took a deep breath and said, "Oh no!" Then she added, "Well now
that you know that . . . I'm not tattling but I don't know where to turn.
I can't bear what I know. Did you know Joan is on sopers?"

And I said, "What are those?"

"Quaaludes. Sleeping pills."

"Why? Can't she sleep?"

"She takes them in the daytime, too. They take them for kicks."

"But why? They make you feel so awful."

"They don't make you feel awful if you make yourself stay awake."

I still had trouble trying to understand this, and then came the crown-
ing blow. She said, "Mama, she not only takes them, but she's been
shooting stuff."

And I got up from the table and I went out of the house and I just
walked up and down the street in that cold air and I kept thinking, What
do I think about? How do I feel? And I didn't feel anything except this
big blank horror. I didn't think, What is she doing to herself, what is she
doing to me. It was just the most appalling concept, and I had to deal
with that concept before I could take it any further.

And then as I got on my last leg back up the street I passed Judge

Donnelly's house and I stood there at his house for a long time . . . thinking, Shall I go and knock on his door and ask him, tell him and say, What does anybody do? If anybody knows anything about drugs and the consequences and what can be done before it goes too far, he might know—being a judge. But then I couldn't take that step and take it to a stranger—even a neighbor stranger. It had to be kept just within the family and just within me until I could really deal with it and accept it.

And then I went through . . . all kinds of things during the next few months. At night I would go to bed thinking, this isn't true, I'm living in a nightmare. I would wake up thinking what is this heavy heartbreak I feel? Who died? Remembrance would strike my heart with a thud. Then I got into the "How could you do this to me" thing. Finally, I got on the right track. "You stupid, how can you do this to yourself?" And then, of course, the arrest and the jail and the going to visit her.

When she was arrested, she was riding in a car with that damned boyfriend of hers and another couple. They were in S____ about 150 miles from here. A cop stopped the car because one of the rear lights was out. But when he saw these kids (Joan and Gary) asleep in the back seat and he smelled liquor, he said, everybody get out. Joan was so deep under the influence that she never did come to, even through the search. By this time I don't know what she was on. . . . They found a bottle of capsules in her purse and some joints. Joan of course utterly denied it . . . "they were planted . . . they weren't on me." But I've found out to my regret that these junkies are all alike—you can't trust them for a minute. And it doesn't matter what they're on, even pot. I've learned over the time not to be so gullible. They stayed in jail overnight. God, what a night that was! We went up the next morning. I talked to the doctor there in town who was also the jail doctor. Very nice man. They had taken her to a kind of recovery place. He suggested that we leave her there until she dried out. He said she was in an awfully dangerous state . . . coming off barbiturates is much harder and more dangerous than practically anything. He said that he would check on her every day. He was such a sweet guy. "Why don't you call up the Probation Department of your local police station," he said. . . . "They can put you onto some group meetings with parents who share your trouble. It will help you." And so finally at the end of six weeks the doctor called me and said, "She's OK and it's been long enough that she's been off them, now it's up to her. If she doesn't take that first one she's going to be OK."

So I went up and brought her home. I didn't go to those parents' meetings. I knew that after that experience Joan was cured. She didn't go out at all at first—she said, "How can I know if I can?" Then finally one day she said, "I'm going out, now I know I can do it. I know I can and it feels good. . . ."

So she went out with that damned Gary at seven o'clock in the evening and I didn't see her again until one o'clock the following day when a car drove up and they rolled Joan out of the car and dragged her into the house and I could tell that she had overdosed. God, what a mess. She had evidently wet her pants and been sick—ugh—I was so ashamed for her.

After that experience I just walked around in a dream—one day I started to cry and couldn't stop. You wouldn't believe it. There I was in the supermarket crying, crying. A neighbor I hardly knew came up to help me—I couldn't really say much to her. She took me out of the supermarket and walked me to a doctor's office—a psychiatrist. That's how I started going to Dr. Casey.

So Joan wasn't really off drugs—she said she was but it never lasted. My hopes went up and down like the tide. I would believe she meant it and then the next day my hopes would be dashed.

I'd thought of drug counseling or therapy, and tried to get her into that good program in L____ county. But admission must be voluntary and she kept denying that she had a drug problem. And they can walk right out the next day if they want to. I didn't know what to do, and I guess I handled it very badly. We had terrible screaming and yelling scenes and I would threaten to have her committed. That, of course, turned her definitely against seeking any help.

She would go out and come home stumbling and reeling. Her sister and brother would try to get her to bed before I saw her. They would be practically carrying her up the stairs. She was disheveled, incoherent, wetting her pants. Of course I never got a full night's sleep. I had the alarm set for every two hours. I always had coffee on the stove and if I was up when she came in I would try to have her drink coffee before she went to bed. If I missed her I'd go to her room to check on her breathing. You can tell by the breathing whether she'd taken an overdose. I didn't know what pills she was taking or shooting, but I do know it was about ten to fourteen a day.

There was her disposition, too. Life was pretty grim at home. It's a wonder we all weathered that year. Bob was working so hard and under such pressure. It was the other two in the family I guess that got us through. They were so helpful and protective of both Joan and me. Trying not to let me know, helping her dress and undress. And Suzie wept over her. She was not eating right, of course, and she was snarly and short-tempered and incoherent. You couldn't talk rationally to her. Of course, she was terribly depressed, too, which got worse, worse, worse until she deliberately overdosed. By that time she was taking so much stuff and there was no way to stop her.

Last June when Mrs. Stiger came up the street to tell me that Joan was down at St. Joseph's Hospital I thought . . . Well, it's good someone else found her, I'd have left her. I'd have just left her. Because she had that year . . . and her answer was that this was what we were going to look forward to. As it turned out, it's fortunate that someone else found her. She had become so depressed that she took a bottle of pills and drove down to the beach to wait for the end. Mrs. Stiger recognized her little VW and thought it was parked kind of funny. She got out and there was Joan—unconscious and alone. A note saying I'm sorry but I'm just too depressed. The doctor at the hospital said it was a chemical depression. You can't keep taking downers and not feel depressed. As it turned out, that was the beginning of the end of it for Joan. After talking to the psychiatrist and to the social worker at the hospital, she decided to see a psychiatrist. When she came home she called up a doctor whose name she had been given at the hospital and saw him about ten times. Then she decided she could do it on her own, and she hasn't had a pill since. Oh, I think she smokes a joint once in a while when she's out to a party, but no more downers.

As to Gary, I haven't even seen that bum around in the last few weeks. He and Joan and a pal of his, Oliver, hung out together. I found Oliver was the one who got the pills. He knew some source and he'd get a supply and peddle them around. It was last summer, after the episode with Joan, that Oliver and another guy, Jimmy, were down at the beach shooting dope and started home. Another kid's parent saw them start around a curve. Oliver drove like a madman anyway. He had a souped-up sports-car that he screamed around in. I guess he didn't straighten out the car quickly enough on the curve and it turned over and Jimmy was killed. Oliver got a broken arm and lost a few teeth—he was the one that should have died, he was no good from way back. In fact, he called the house one time after that. "Is Joan home?" he said. And I said, "Who is this?" And he said "Oliver" and I said, "How do you dare to call this house you Goddamn junkie." I said, "Don't you dare call and slime up my house." I said, "If you want to see Joan you wait till she's out and about and you run into her, but don't you dare call here." And he said, "Well, geez, Mrs. Rampert," and I said, "Oh geez, Mrs. Rampert my foot." I said " . . . the only thing I can wonder is why the hell didn't you die that day Jimmy died, you should have. The world would have been a lot better off without you." I couldn't keep my mouth shut.

A few weeks later I happened to glance out the bedroom window. I looked out and there were those two creeps, Gary and Oliver, going down the driveway with their arms full of records. The family room is on the floor below.

"Where do you think you're going," I yelled out.

"Downstairs to listen to records with Joan."

And I thought, is that so? So I tore out of my bedroom and I ran into the living room and I grabbed the firepoker and I went down the stairs and around to the back door and I threw it open and I said, "Get the hell out of here you Goddamned junkies. Where do you think you're going?" "Well, Joan invited us over, we're going to play records." And I said, "That's what you think, get out of here. Don't you ever come around this house again, get out." They started up the driveway and me running after them with this poker. And one says, "Don't you threaten me with that thing, lady." And I said, "Who the hell's threatening you, I'm going to kill you."

They haven't been back.

Well, Joan is back at school now and has real career plans. I don't think she'll go back down that road. She's so different now, so gay—vibrant—funny. Junkies are so dull—I still classify in my mind anyone who takes any kind of drugs as a junkie. They're totally narcissistic, there's no compassion, no humor, no humor at all. Oh, they'll laugh mechanically, but humor, wit—none.

And after all, I can even think of Gary more kindly now. He's off the dope, too, but they don't see much of each other anymore. He was really very protective of Joan. He never let another guy near her. I've heard Johnnie, my son, and his friends talking about loose chicks—and don't the boys love to see the loose chicks getting high on alcohol or pills. There was a party not long ago . . . call a gathering like that a party! One of the boys was telling me about it. He said they had beer, but someone was passing out sopers. He said, "Wow, the girls were taking them like they were going out of style" and he laughed. I was appalled when he followed up his laughter with the statement that there was one girl, course she's loose anyway, but he said fifteen guys . . . and she didn't even know about any but the first two. They go to the parties and take pills or get drunk. They know they're going to get laid and they don't care . . . to know about it . . . these girls don't care . . . they don't get money for it so there's no prostitution involved.

One thing Joan did for the other two—they won't go down that road. Maybe they'll do other things, but it won't be drugs or alcohol. They don't even want to take drugs that are prescribed, and Johnnie sticks to his two beers.

I: Do you ever feel responsible?

M: Oh, briefly, I think. You know, one night Bob and I sat with Joan until 3:30 in the morning talking about her involvement, the reason why. "Is your life so painful that you have to resort to pain-killers? If it is, we can soul-search and we can change. We can do whatever is necessary to be done that your life not be that painful." And that's when she said " . . . I love my home and I have two parents I think are just great, I'm envied my parents . . ." and that's when it all came spilling out: She didn't like moving around so much a long time ago when she was growing up. I wrestled with that one. I thought, Oh Lord, if I hadn't married a man who was ambitious and if we hadn't moved around. Yeah, but I did, and we did move around. And it's all accomplished and it's done and it's over and if Joan is bearing scars from this there are places she can go, there are things that she can do to ease those scars. And she doesn't have to take those pills. . . . No, I don't feel responsible. But I don't understand it. She always seemed so easygoing, so poised. She made friends so easily . . . we thought. She said it took her two years to get comfortable with a friend and that just as she was easing into it, we'd move. When we came here she was going into her junior year in high school. She was even elected secretary of her class. I thought everything was just fine for her. She's so pretty—and intelligent, too. Last year when they tested her in that recovery center they said her IQ was 134. But the reason she was elected secretary of her class was because she was in with this drug group. She belonged. Then she didn't want to go away to college. But we insisted. It was only a hundred miles but it seemed as though she was home every weekend. If I had known how hard it was for her to go away to college . . . I wouldn't have insisted. But in my family we always went *away* to college. Well now she's going to the local junior college and next year she talks about going to the university. She's so close to self-pride and that feeling that there's nothing else like accomplishment . . . she wants to study criminology! But she'll live at home if she wants to.

Now when I look at her I'm quietly pleased . . . I smile a lot. And she does, too.

Fighting for
What's Right

ET up off your ass and fight for what you have a right to fight for. . . . People are deficient in rights, and they have every right in the world to get them." The speaker was urging his fellow students at a western university to join in a strike. The Black Students Union had presented to the officials of the college ten demands focusing upon a black studies program to be a department of the college but under the management of the blacks. The college had initiated some black studies but had refused to give control of the program to students. Whereupon, the students went on strike.

The motivations of the black students were revealed in further statements by them: "We're talking about people's needs. We blacks are a servile people. We have no background, no heritage. We want to know what's important in society, in culture, for you as a person. The universities are sterile. They don't have substance to relate to. We want to learn about ourselves, not how to be automatons. We want to be ourselves, human beings, not the economic man. If you recognize those needs, how are you going to act to get them satisfied? Our aim is to get power, and until the students get power, everything else is bullshit."

Would you join in this type of student strike? On one side of this question would be the desire to assist black people to achieve their aspirations, and to go along with the students who were pressing you to strike; and on the other side is the interference of a strike with the pursuit of your education, the potential damage to the institution from disruptive acts, and the probable deterioration of an academic program if its direction were transferred from the faculty and administration to the students.

Should you become involved in any political activism or campus activism or campus activities? You have the options: You can stay with your studies, resisting the temptations and the pressures of your peers to join in the action; or you can become part of the action.

The arguments for the first alternative are obvious: You came to college to get an education, you have a limited number of years in which to do it, you may not have sufficient money to permit you to take time out for campus activities, and you may not agree fully with the aims of the activist leaders. Perhaps the more extreme forms of student agitation just don't appeal to you. Perhaps you distrust the leaders, some of whom may be agitators from off campus.

On the other hand, the arguments for joining in political action can be potent. You may have strong feelings that American ideals are being undermined in our society, that the values that dominate our life today need to be changed, that the college is not genuinely responsive to students' needs. You may have convictions that as a consumer and a citizen you have responsibilities to act on political issues—in college as well as later. If no one protests the actions of those who wield power, what kind of society will eventuate? There is also the contention that participation in politics, social action, and governmental activities will provide educative experiences for you.

College students of today express considerable awareness of the maladjustments that have been appearing in our society. We have concrete evidence of their beliefs from the ACE survey of freshman women. The following data show the norms of their beliefs:

	Percent who believe the statement
The Federal Government is not doing enough to control environmental pollution	90.8
The Federal Government is not doing enough to protect the consumer from faulty goods and services	77.2
All young people should have the opportunity to go to college	70.8

	Percent who believe the statement
People should be discouraged from having large families	67.5
The Federal Government is not doing enough to promote school desegregation	53.0
There is too much concern in the courts for the rights of criminals	41.1
Marijuana should be legalized	35.0

The students also believe that social action is necessary. The SCOPE survey of freshman women revealed that they believe that student protest movements are important because they draw attention to the evils in society. Fifty-four percent so believe, although many do so with reservations. A large portion, 64 percent, think that if we are to survive in our environment, we will have to deny ourselves many things that we now think are necessities. Almost as many, 58 percent, said that it is more important to work for the good of the community than for one's own self-interest. Those who disagree with these statements are fewer than a third, and only a small group feel strongly in disagreement.

College-age youth have been persuasive in getting a number of significant social and educational changes made. The voting age has been lowered to eighteen. The agitation of youth against the Vietnam War helped to shift American opinion about the war. Undoubtedly youth have made us all more sensitive about racism, poverty, and pollutions. They have revolutionized attitudes toward sex. They have persuaded the colleges, several hundred of them, to initiate ethnic studies programs. They have stimulated medical and law schools to seek black and Chicano students, and also women, in larger numbers.

Looking back in history, it can be seen that student political movements had led in effecting profound changes in the world. According to Seymour M. Lipset (*Daedalus,* Winter 1968, p. 344):

Students were a key element in the revolutions of 1848 in Germany and Austria, and student activism stimulated the "professors parliament" which almost succeeded in toppling several monarchs. In czarist Russia, students spearheaded various revolutionary movements, and the university campus was a major center of revolutionary activity. In the East European countries, where education was limited to a small proportion of the population, students were often the carriers of modern ideas of liberty, socialism, industrialization, and equality of opportunity. The important role of students in the movements for national independence in the developing areas also goes back a half century or more. In imperial

China, students were crucial to the imperial effort at modernization but at the same time spread republican and radical ideas throughout the society. Students helped overthrow the dynasty in 1911 and were thereafter one of the elements continually pushing China toward modernization and radical ideologies. In other Asian and African countries, students were often a central element in anticolonial struggles.

But students have sometimes chosen to back a movement that was antisocial, as for example, the Nazis in Germany. This suggests that the goals of the students should be clear, and that they should be humanistic rather than merely to gain power.

Students have been pressing for a share in making decisions about the general policies and the academic programs of the colleges. A national survey of students revealed that the demand for participation in the governance of the colleges topped the list of interests.

The student drives for participation have been partially successful. The most surprising dent has been the admission of students as members of Boards of Trustees or Regents. The number of instances is small, and the number of students is small, but the door has been opened! Another valuable type of participation has become possible in those colleges that have adopted an all-college senate. The senate is usually composed of selected, often elected representatives of faculty, students and administrators. In view of the fact that the senate usually makes major decisions of academic policy, this is an important development. The gain in student participation on faculty-student committees in the academic departments, which has been the largest, has great value. It is within the departments where the major share of the decisions about the educational program and the teaching are made.

The judicial proceedings on the campuses have been undergoing radical transformation. Encouraged by court decisions about their civil rights, students have achieved on most campuses the right to due process when they become subjected to discipline. Arbitrary disciplines and dismissals are no longer tolerated by the courts. Due process includes the right of a student who has been accused of something to see the specific charges, to be represented by an attorney, to have a fair hearing, and after a decision, the right of appeal. A statement on students' rights has been agreed upon by the National Students Association and several associations representing the colleges and universities. It should be easy for you to get a copy.

How far can a college go in involving students in its decision-making? One view is that students are the recipients of the education provided for them and they do not have competence to judge what the content or the methods should be. Furthermore, they are transients in that they remain at the college a few years at most; they should not be permitted to impose policies on those who do remain. The opposite view is that the students are the consumers of education and as consumers should have a voice. It is they who receive the outlines of courses and can judge how adequately a course has been planned; who listen to lectures and can tell a motivating, effective presentation from a dull, wandering one; who are then evaluated and can recognize whether the evaluation related to the objectives planned for the course. They have personal reactions as to whether the courses meet their needs. They also live more closely within the environment of the college and can offer ideas for its improvement. Their awareness of the social issues, especially of social injustices, is strong. The balance of arguments weighs in favor of student participation. The participation, however, needs to relate both to student interests and rights and also to their ability to contribute in making wise decisions.

A college is essentially a two-phased organization. One is the academic program, the other is the community of people living and working together. The academic program is staffed by professional people. They have been employed because of their professional attainments and expertise. It is in the interests of everyone, including the students, to have the academic planning and teaching well done. Students have valuable contributions to make on aspects of the program, but the faculty have much more. The effort should be a cooperative one, but the faculty have a professional responsibility that they should not relinquish. They should retain control. In community affairs, however, the students are close to the problems and have competence as citizens; hence their representation in decision making on these matters should be large.

Assuming that you want to become a participant in political action and in influencing the college to make good decisions about its program, which method of group pressure is best for you to join? What type of mass social action is most effective in producing the desired type of change?

One set of alternatives is between violent and nonviolent techniques. A lesson may be drawn from the disruption and violence practiced by dissident students during the 1965–72 period. The combative tactics that were used overshadowed the good ones. In addition to peaceful picketing and demonstrations, the strikers broke windows, set fires, set off bombs, disrupted classes, attacked professors, used insulting language, and attempted to overpower the police. They could have foreseen that the colleges and the state would use force against force and would be able to command stronger resources in power than the students could possibly assemble. By using such tactics, the students lost friends who might have helped them and alienated a large portion of the public.

Massive demonstrations are a good way to get attention directed toward a problem. But they do not have to be violent. The American Civil Liberties Union, which has a good record in defending the rights of individuals to protest their grievances, draws a distinction between peaceful demonstrations and disruptions:

Picketing, demonstrations, sit-ins, or student strikes, provided they are conducted in an orderly and nonobstructive manner, are a legitimate mode of expression, whether politically motivated or directed against the college administration, and should not be prohibited. Demonstrators, however, have no right to deprive others of the opportunity to speak or be heard; take hostages; physically obstruct the movement of others; or otherwise disrupt the educational or institutional processes in a way that interferes with the safety or freedom of others.

Dissent is protected by the First Amendment to the Federal Constitution, hence the courts will shield the persons engaged in it. Disruption is not protected. The democratic way includes the use of demonstrations but not violence. A college is normally a democratic institution. The people who compose it are people of good will accustomed to rational procedures, not to force. The faculty have a strong empathy toward students. They exist and do their work for the ultimate benefit of the students.

The method that is most effective in dealing with faculty, and also with the administration, is persuasion. To persuade others about the need for change, it is necessary to amass information that will be impressive, and create continuous pressures in support of the request. The primary technique is negotiation, but demonstrations may be important to use as added pressure.

Mark Rudd, an articulate student leader at Columbia University, had a good opportunity to persuade the faculty to the student view, but he blew it. He had been invited to speak to the faculty. Some of the faculty were as disturbed as the students by the decision to put a new gymnasium in a park used by the people of the area. By using the right tactics, Mark could have enlarged the number of faculty who would join with the student protesters. But he belligerently accused the faculty of talking only bullshit, haranguing them instead of discussing the problem persuasively. He did not take account of the rationality of professors and of their training in making objective approaches to problems. He turned faculty off instead of on.

Although considerable progress has been made on a few fronts, many of the political and social problems identified by youth are resistant to rapid change. The attempt to find solutions must be pursued over many years. For example, the movement for women's liberation, under way for more than a century, has made some gains, but there is still much work to do. The gains made while you are a student need to be enlarged and consolidated after you have left college. Consequently, an objective of the college years should be to prepare yourself well for future community participation and political action.

This means that students while in college should train themselves in the skills and habits of participation. Continued activity after college will depend on the degree that skills learned in early life are perfected and actions built into habits.

With some effort, a woman can ferret out courses that will provide her with concepts, increased verbal facility, reasoning abilitities, and in some cases with skills for relating to other people. Most of these courses will be found in the psychosociological area, but not all. Other courses would be in political science, in writing and speaking skills, in history, in logic and mathematics, to name some.

How will you determine the values that underlie your decisions to promote a cause or oppose an action? If you do not have a considered basis for selecting the good, you may scrap the good with the bad. Take, for example, the value of honesty. Honesty leads to personal integrity. Respect for the rights of others seems to be a better principle of action than the claim that the ends justify the means. It may be argued that those who rip off things are in need and therefore stealing is justified, or that it is stealing from the establishment who got theirs dishonestly. But when a shoplifter robs a store, the store passes the costs to the consumer —thus it is the poor to whom higher prices are a burden who suffer most. On the Berkeley campus of the University of California, in 1971 there were 2005, and in 1972, 1515 instances of theft reported. In 1971, 400 bicycles were stolen. At one small college, where honesty in all relationships was formerly the prevailing tone, today, as a result of book pilfering, stealing money from purses and typewriters from rooms, the situation has changed to constant watchfulness and locked doors. Dishonesty leads to personal distrust and to social chaos. It also means more police.

Another example of a desirable quality in human relationships is tolerance of the views and rights of others. Political freedom in the United States depends upon tolerance of the views and rights of others. The value of tolerance has been brought into question by some theorists, and one can agree that there are injustices that a society should not tolerate. Some youth feel that they have not been listened to, and so they drown out the voices of others who speak. However, those who shout down a speaker because the views differ from their own will be planting the seeds of intolerance, and they may be the next victim.

It is not too difficult to let your hair grow long, but how do you change beliefs? If you desire to reform the values by which people live, an essential step while in college is to study values, existing and potential, in order to have a comprehensive view of them and to arrive at well-founded beliefs and commitments. It is also essential to weave the new values into your own life-style.

The study of values is a continuous process of examining theories advanced by learned men, plus the concepts that are the foundations for political, social, and economic activity, and then making your own evaluation of them. The views of philosophers are not necessarily right, but these persons have given intensive thought to ideas and ideals. Their thoughts can be stimulating to your own.

In other courses you can explore such questions as, what does history reveal about the progress of human society? What contributes to progress and what becomes a stumbling block? What seems to be valid as principles of human behavior? What is uplifting and what is dissipating? What contributes to physical and mental well being, and what does not? What is the most viable type of society?

These questions are intangible and far-reaching, hence difficult. You will not find all the answers in college, but you can make progress in finding them. You can also acquire some of the intellectual tools by which to search further for answers.

Liberation Through Education

HE political freedom of women was secured through the right to vote and hold public office; their sexual freedom has been accelerated by the perfection of contraceptive methods; a degree of economic freedom is being attained for them by expanding the types of careers available to women. Liberation, however, has an additional dimension beyond politics, beyond sex, beyond economic freedom. It is the development of the woman as a person. She will attain this goal as she achieves intellectual competence and preparation to live a full life.

It is at college where you can best work toward this end. A college has as its central purpose to assist students to learn, in general, and to attain competencies of specific kinds. A college woman, after graduation, will differ from other women in the degree to which she has changed, in the degree to which she has used the help of the college in developing her full potentialities as a person.

A college is an environment different from any you have heretofore experienced. It is organized to stimulate you intellectually, to provide educational facilities for your use, and to motivate you to be methodical in your thinking and in training yourself. Through its faculty, books, laboratories, and programs, a college seeks to change you in many ways: to become a person who is observant, reflective, insightful; to become more knowledgeable about yourself, your society, and the world in which you live; to become competent in a vocation; to become more considerate and skillful in interpersonal relations; to cause you to develop for yourself a more matured philosophy of life.

But the studies that have been made of the achievements of students in college usually have shown that they have not really changed very much. The students have graduated with some evidence of achievement, but they have remained substantially the same persons. They have passed their courses one by one, but they have not become the kind of person described as liberated.

If you want to achieve more than the accumulation of credits and of passing grades, it is helpful to work out some educational objectives. This may seem to be a simple task because your main objective may be a single one, such as to prepare yourself for a better job than you otherwise could get. But the opportunity in college is not only to do this, but to achieve much more. In order to take full account of the possibilities at the college, you should make a methodical analysis of possible objectives that relate to your growth as a person. This may include your growth as a liberated woman.

For this self-analysis it is convenient to use a frame of reference that includes the principal facets for planning your education. There are at least four: finding a vocation and preparing for it; improving your cultural knowledge and activities; developing yourself in many personal ways; and refining and maturing your philosophy of life. These four could, of course, be subdivided, and you may add facets consistent with your own perceptions of your needs. In a way, the four facets are four different perspectives of your life; taken together they represent a self-examination of the whole of your personal development.

The many kinds of considerations which need to be taken into account in identifying a career and preparing for it—your interests and aptitudes, types of potential careers and their relative advantages and disadvantages, employment, discrimination against women, and your plans for harmonizing marriage and carreer—have been discussed in Chapters 6, 7, 8, and 9.

The possibilities for cultural development, including the accumulation of knowledge, are almost limitless, much beyond what can be accomplished in four years of college. But doors can be opened, appetites whetted, appreciations expanded and refined, skills of reading, writing and conversation improved, and attitudes and habits changed. The college environment can also influence you to make substantial changes in your interests and tempt you to acquire a considerable foundation of knowledge. The basis for continued cultural growth after college can be laid. The objective of becoming a cultured, knowledgeable person, has been discussed in preceding chapters, especially 4 and 5.

A third possible objective is to develop yourself as a person. This was discussed in Chapter 10, "Who Am I?"; but in defining objectives for yourself, consider these two dimensions: the inner self; and the skills that may accrue as a result of specific training. One educator, Arthur W. Chickering, has itemized the components of personal development as including: understanding yourself, clarifying your purposes, growing in self-confidence, becoming self-governing, understanding others, and developing integrity—that is, causing your actions to be consistent with your words. Examine yourself in the light of these six phases of personal development; identify your greatest strengths and weaknesses, and from these determine your objectives for yourself.

You should also inventory your skills and decide where you will want or need improvements. Everyone benefits generally from physical skills— for health building, for game playing, and for vocational and avocational activities. Among these may be some manual skills that are essential to your vocation. A dentist or a glassblower, an artist or a musician, a typist or a computer operator, all need manual skills to achieve genuine competence. Vocal skills are also important, not only for concert artists and public lecturers or office seekers, but also as a medium for expressing yourself and communicating with other people. The art of thinking requires a developed skill in that it involves the process of analysis and synthesis—a scholar, for example, can be identified by the self-discipline with which she defines a problem, assembles relevant data, controls the variables that may affect her reasoning, makes an analysis and composes the findings with accuracy and precision.

Many young people are concerned about how they relate to other people. A primary objective in personal development can be to enlarge your interpersonal competence. By this is meant the ability to work effectively with others and to develop good rapport between yourself and other people. These are the paths to successful relationships with parents, friends, and in the future with your husband and family. Such training may help you to reduce the generation gap when you have children. Furthermore, good personal relations on a job or with one's clients or patients in a profession are essential for the best success in a career. Skill in interpersonal relations is an essential ingredient in achieving understanding between individuals of different races, cultures and nationalities.

The fourth broad objective for you to consider is to mature your thinking on what life is all about. You may have thought about this a lot, but the college can assist you to think more systematically, and on a philosophical plane. There are the individual and the social aspects; questions of environment and space and time; the evolution of life and the ultimate destiny; the here and now and the future. Will you shed your prejudices in favor of views based upon facts and reasoning? Will you learn how best to reconcile the individual welfare with the social good? Will you achieve some knowledge of the great religions and philosophies in order to shape your own beliefs? Will you sift and weigh the concepts that have been articulated by the women and men who have speculated about the meaning of life? These are the kinds of questions to ask yourself to help you to identify courses to select and professors with whom to explore ideas. Colleges have purposes that are harmonious with various types of personal objectives. They therefore provide counseling, instruction, and experiences that will assist you to achieve your objectives.

A pervasive purpose of all colleges is to develop the intellectual competence of students. Generally speaking, the primary characteristic of the instruction in a college is the use of rational learning. It is assumed that the best attainable knowledge is found through empirical and scientific research. The aim is to get at the best possible evidence to support ideas and theories. The development of the theory of the evolution of life, for example, resulted from the interpretations of the life forms that were found in the successive strata of sedimentary rocks. This was a profound change in view from that described in the Book of Genesis. When Thomas Huxley in 1878 lectured on the new biology—evolution—at Johns Hopkins University, his views created a sensation. They were rejected by the surrounding community, yet the evidence that life had evolved from primitive forms continued to mount. Today, a century later, the theory of evolution is almost universally accepted. Earlier Galileo had recanted his teaching that the earth moved around the sun—the church had forced him to do so—but his telescope proved that he was right. This is the rational way, the use of observations and inductive reasoning as the way to learn, rather than repeating dogma. A college uses rational learning in training the mind.

Another purpose of any college is to assist you to gain better perspectives, for example, historical perspective. The light that is shed on human development by the evidence found through studying the geologic ages has been mentioned. An illustration that involves a much shorter span of time is the development of the concept of civil liberties—freedom of speech, association, and religious expression. Although we all know that the first ten amendments to the federal constitution protect these freedoms, it helps in understanding their full significance and how precious they are to trace the struggles through which they were evolved beginning with the Magna Carta. Still another example derives from the scientific investigations that began when Lavoisier and Priestly discovered oxygen in the eighteenth century, continued when later scientists identified other elements, and finally reached a climax when the tremendous energy that is in the atom was unlocked. Our knowledge of nuclear physics was not the result of sudden inspiration or invention, but instead is an accumulation of discoveries over two centuries, each in turn dependent upon the previous one. Of immediate relevance to you as a woman is perspective relating to the role of women. Traditional views about women assigned to them a role secondary to men, and subordinate to their husbands. But in the twentieth century they have been achieving liberation, and today they are making gains toward attaining equality of status with men. The ability to look at all things in perspective is one of the marks of a well-educated person.

A college also aims to help a student achieve breadth of view and depth of knowledge. Breadth helps to lift the student out of narrow channels into wider horizons. It introduces her to subjects that represent a pattern of existing knowledge. It acquaints her with a variety of vocations and professions so that her choice will be unlimited. It opens windows on the several great cultures in the world—Eastern, African, Western. Breadth of cultural understanding leads to richer life experiences through enjoying history, literature, art, music, science. It also is of value in creating good intercultural relations.

One aspect of breadth is an acquaintance with one's physical environment. For this purpose most colleges put considerable curricular emphasis upon the natural sciences. Always of importance in discovering as much as we can about the earth, the living things that inhabit it, and the utilization, conservation, and management of its resources, this study is doubly important in this age of the dissipation of our natural resources and the pollution of our environment. The explorations in space have stimulated the imaginations of us all; the college can make available to us the most recent findings in space and any fresh theories about the other planets, various solar systems, and the origins of matter and energy.

Most colleges also teach in depth. This is to help you penetrate more fully at least one field of knowledge to assist you with preparation for a specialization. It is a way of training you for a career, whether a vocation or a profession. It also provides you with the concepts, principles, and tools to carry on in more advanced study or in your career.

Some colleges aim to prepare students for social action. Most institutions are limited in their ability to engage in direct social action but they are nevertheless agents for social change. This is because the institution continually probes for fresh light on social problems, publishes the findings, gives to faculty and students a large degree of freedom to act, and prepares graduates to have a greater degree of competence for social action. The interested student can find many courses that will supply background knowledge, and training experiences that will provide her with skills for social action. Some of the resources were described in Chapter 19. Skills are especially needed by those who are motivated to help reduce the ills of society. They are needed by one who desires to become an effective person—one who, because of her perspective of history, her critical observation of contemporary society, and her understanding of social dynamics helps to facilitate needed change in the world.

The development of your inner self—feelings of security, self-confidence, ability to manage your own affairs, and so forth—takes place as you mature, and as you gain knowledge about yourself. The college can give you much help along the way through courses and activities that develop you physically and emotionally—especially courses in psychology, philosophy, and physical education. But your growth will also take place naturally as you pass from adolescence into adulthood and as you assimilate your education, letting fresh ideas and new skills change your perceptions of life and your activities. All of the intellectual experiences you have at the college will help you to develop your mind, and all of the experiences, intellectual and personal, will assist you to develop yourself as a person.

Though you examine yourself from various perspectives, such as the four we have discussed, you are nevertheless a whole person. Life has unity and needs to be considered as a whole. The college can help you to see yourself as a whole. The most important goal in college is to work out a philosophy for one's life. This is something you do as you integrate the various phases of your education in order to become a liberated woman.

People who desire liberation need to acquire the tools of learning and the techniques of action: the ability to verbalize, to calculate, to analyze and synthesize, to create, to organize, and to administer. They need to free themselves from irrational prejudices, religious and political bigotry, and remedial diseases. They need to learn how to organize into social groups to secure, on the basis of equality of opportunity for all persons, such advantages as physical comfort, health services, educational opportunity, economic justice, peaceful relations with other social and political groups, and some leisure time for cultural pursuits. These aims are consistent with those of a college and indeed lie at the heart of the college program.

College will assist you to refine the values that govern your life. Insights into values are to be found through analyzing human experience to see what kinds of actions have been good for human beings. Out of the experience of the human race, people learn to set up value scales such as justice and injustice, temperance and intemperance, goodwill and ill will, honesty and dishonesty, on which actions can be contrasted and weighed. A college provides many courses in history, literature, art, religion, economics, anthropology, sociology and philosophy, that describe, interpret, and evaluate human experience. Through making your own evaluations, you can determine the values by which you will live and chart your actions. The tools of learning, the techniques of action, and the value scales for action are components of the education that will help you to become liberated.

Liberation in its highest sense means becoming the master of yourself. It means freeing yourself from the bondage of the trivial and the immediate. It means fresh perceptions about yourself, who you are, and what your potentialities are. It means new and broader horizons for your thinking about life, about your fellow women and men, about the world in which you live. It means having the sense of security that comes with the possession of knowledge about yourself, about human life, about your environment. It means learning to utilize harmoniously and creatively your abilities—intellectual, physical, and emotional. It means creating within yourself a confidence that you can plan and live a life that will satisfy you.

Liberation also means joining with others in freeing individuals as social beings. This means becoming master of nature through understanding nature, harnessing its forces, and yet conserving life and energies. It means joining with others in freeing mankind, but more especially womankind, from traditions and customs that may be obsolete or that may unnecessarily inhibit individual freedoms. It means learning how to plan for social progress in a way that will achieve the greatest possible human well-being. It means developing an ethical basis for governing one's actions as they affect others.

A woman in college is at the threshold of the finest years of her life. What does life mean to you? What kind of person will you be? What will be your goals? What are the intellectual and physical competencies that you should have to carry out your aims? These are some of the questions to ask yourself as you proceed with your education. For a primary purpose of education is to assist you to grasp the meaning of life.

References and Suggestions for Reading

Index

References and Suggestions for Reading

The Education of Women

McGuigan, Dorothy Dies. *A Dangerous Experiment.* Ann Arbor, Michigan: The University of Michigan, Center for Continuing Education of Women, 1970. An account of the struggle that one university had in persuading itself that women are as educable as men and deserve equal opportunity.

Stone, James C., and DeNevi, Donald P. *Portraits of the American University, 1890–1910.* San Francisco: Jossey-Bass, 1971. A choice collection of journal articles about higher education as it is used to be, also many pictures. Some of the articles discuss the care of women students and how they should be educated in college.

Woody, Thomas. *A History of Women's Education in the United States,* 2 vols. New York: The Science Press, 1929. A well-documented history that gives detailed information about the earlier beliefs concerning the physical and psychological limitations of women, female seminaries, ladies' courses, chaperon requirements, and also about the gradual achievement by women of equal treatment with men in college.

Different Types of College Programs

Eddy, Edward D., Jr. *Colleges of Our Land and Time.* New York: Harper and Row, 1957. A portrayal of the evolution of the colleges of agriculture and of engineering, and of value in explaining why education for various careers is so important in the United States.

Glazer, Edmund J., Jr. *This Is the Community College*. Boston: Houghton Mifflin Co., 1968.

A description of community-junior colleges and their programs. Paperback.

Henderson, Algo D. *The Innovative Spirit*. San Francisco: Jossey-Bass, 1970.

Although written for educators, this book contains many descriptions of new experiments among the colleges and universities and suggests ideas for change.

Schmidt, George H. *The Liberal Arts College*. New Brunswick, N.J.: Rutgers University Press, 1957.

The purpose of a liberal education and the role of the liberal arts colleges in providing this kind of education.

Career Opportunities

Folger, John K. and others. *Human Resources and Higher Education*. New York: Russell Sage Foundation, 1970.

A study of the needs for educated personnel. Detailed information is given about the opportunities in selected fields such as teaching, nursing, social welfare, and medicine. One chapter is devoted to the education and vocational development of women.

Gore, Alice. *Career Opportunities for Women in Business*. New York: E. P. Dutton and Co., 1963.

Brief descriptions of twenty-one occupational fields, mostly in business, but including government. An advantage of the book is its breakdown of specific opportunities for women. Advice about getting a job.

Occupational Outlook Handbook. Washington: United States Department of Labor, Bureau of Labor Statistics, Bulletin 1700, 1972-73, or latest edition. Provides information on more than eight hundred occupations; also in each instance, references through which more information can be obtained are given.

Discriminations and Dilemmas

Epstein, Cynthia Fuchs. *Woman's Place, Options and Limits in Professional Careers*. Berkeley: University of California Press, 1970.

An objective discussion of woman's place, but also provocative in picturing vividly the many discriminations and dilemmas that confront educated women when seeking fulfillment in a career.

Pogrebin, Lottie Cottin. *How To Make It in a Man's World*. Garden City, N.Y.: Doubleday and Co., 1970.

get along with men in the business world.

Identity

Bardwick, Judith M. *Psychology of Women.* New York: Harper and Row, 1971.
A middle-of-the-road inquiry into the psychology of women vis-à-vis men. Bardwick believes sex differences originate in the differences in the reproductive system. She also posits that there are basic psychological differences (particularly independence and aggression), organization of their egos, and motives and goals between men and women.

Edson, W. Doyle. ''An Analysis of Identity from the Standpoint of Erikson, Freud, Kroeber and Tillich.'' Unpublished Ph.D. dissertation, Claremont Graduate School, 1968.
A succinct, clear, and readable analysis of this complex subject.

Erikson, Erik H. *Identity, Youth and Crisis.* New York: W. W. Norton & Co., 1968.
An erudite exposition of identity, its formation through the epigenetic principle and specific stages and the individual's interaction with the society.

Sex

Boston Women's Health Book Collective. *Our Bodies, Ourselves. A Book By and For Women.* New York: Simon and Schuster, 1971.
One summer a group of women decided to study the female body. This excellent book is the result. Carefully researched from textbooks, medical journals, and women's experiences, it became more than a book about female physiology. It includes also sexuality, nutrition, childbearing and health care generally. It makes women aware of their socialization and what it means to be female. It informs women about themselves.

Farnsworth, Dana L. ''Sexual Morality: Campus Dilemma.'' *International Psychiatric Clinics,* 7 (1970), 133-151.
Discusses new sexual code of college students with respect to advantages, disadvantages, and dangers. Role of college in developing responsible behavior in students.

Freeman, Harrup A., and Freeman, Ruth S. ''Senior College Women: Their Sexual Standards and Activity, Parts I and II.'' *NAWDC Journal,* 29, (Spring and Winter 1966), 59-64, 136-143.
Reports the results of three studies, from 1962-66, regarding behavior and standards of college women: whom they seek for counseling, the people and institutions that influence them, and their dating, love, and sexual experiences.

Hall, Patricia L., and Wagner, Nathaniel H. ''Initial Heterosexual Experience in

Sweden and the United States: A Cross-Cultural Survey." *Proceedings, 80th Annual Convention, APA,* 1972, pp. 293-94.

Kantner, John F., and Zelnick, Melvin. "Sexual Experience of Young Unmarried Women in the United States." *Family Planning Perspectives,* 4, October 1972

Katz, Joseph J. and Associates. *No Time for Youth: Growth and Constraint in College Students.* San Francisco: Jossey-Bass, 1968.
Interesting, well-written report of a study of the development of college students over a four-year period.

Lowry, Pamela. "Unwanted Pregnancy—Why?" Oakland: Planned Parenthood/World Population. Mimeo. (Also appeared in *Harvard Crimson,* Aug. 10, 1971).

Packard, Vance. *The Sexual Wilderness.* New York: David McKay, 1968. Pocket Book edition, 1970.

Planned Parenthood/World Population pamphlets: *Birth Control.* New York: Family Planning Resources Center, 1971.
Contraceptive Effectiveness. Oakland, Ca. (mimeo.)
Modern Methods of Birth Control. New York: Planned Parenthood Federation of America, 1965. Rev. 1970.

Drugs

Blum, Richard H. and Associates. *Students and Drugs.* San Francisco: Jossey-Bass, 1970.
Reports on the psychoactive drugs used by high school and college students. The broad scope of this book includes the history of drug use, who uses drugs, why, the psychological and educational effects, motivations and lifestyles of drug users.

Brecker, Edward M., and the Editors of Consumer Reports. *Licit and Illicit Drugs.* Mt. Vernon, N.Y.: Consumers Union, 1972.

Coles, Robert; Brenner, Joseph H.; and Meagher, Dermot. *Drugs and Youth.* New York: Liveright Publishing Corp., 1970.
Excellent, readable, factual discourse of the medical, psychiatric, and legal facts of drugs and drug usage by college students.

Hollister, Leo E. "Marihuana in Man: Three Years Later." *Science* 172 (April 2, 1971), 21-29.
Reviews the literature of the past three years regarding the physical and mental effects of marihuana with brief history of man's use in the past. Good review of current information.

U.S. Report to the U.S. Congress from the Secretary of Health, Education, and Welfare. *Alcohol and Health.* Washington: U.S. Government Printing Office, 1970.

First special report summarizing current knowledge of the effects of using and abusing alcoholic beverages. Considers alcoholism in category of disease and covers physical, psychological and social causes of abuse and their effects as presently known. Present research findings are presented and areas of future needs discussed.

U.S. Report to the U.S. Congress from the Secretary of Health, Education, and Welfare. *Marihuana and Health.* Washington: U.S. Government Printing Office, 1971.

Second of annual reports to be submitted to Congress in accordance with the "Marihuana and Health Reporting Act." Summarizes current status of physical and psychological consequences of marihuana use. Balanced objective reporting.

Social Action on Campus

Avorn, Jerry L. and others. *Up Against the Ivy Wall.* New York: Atheneum, 1969.

Numerous articles and books have been written by students about the student demonstrations during 1964–70. This one is descriptive of the disruption at Columbia University during 1968.

Carnegie Commission on Higher Education. *Dissent and Disruption.* New York: McGraw-Hill, 1971.

An analysis of student activism, mostly from the point of view of the institutions. Dissent is appropriate, but disruptions and violence cause backlashes and may defeat the objectives of the disrupters.

"Students and Politics," *Daedalus* (Winter, 1968).

This journal contains sixteen articles by sociologists and political scientists on student activism in various countries of the world.

178

Index